the
early
voters

MILES HOWARD

FIRST EDITION, OCTOBER 2017

Cover design and chapter photographs by Miles Howard

Author photograph by Julia Howard

The Cataloging-in-Publication Data is on file at the Library of Congress

ISBN 978-0-9995418-0-7

Printed in the United States of America
10 9 8 7 6 5 4 3 2 1

To George,
for teaching me how to talk with strangers.

CONTENTS

INTRODUCTION

This book is a collection of stories about being young, anxious, and full of unrealized dreams.

But in order to tell these stories, I have to begin with my own.

THE WAVE

It was June 10, 2012, roughly four years after the U.S. housing market imploded. There was a party that night. I had to be there.

The soiree was happening at a new lounge in South Boston surreptitiously called "Happy's." It was the kind of place where you could order a $15 bowl of Matzo ball soup and chase it with a $7.50 tallboy of PBR. The music was strictly Top 40, nobody danced, and the interior was described as "Postmodern Berlin Meets *Leave It To Beaver*." Places like Happy's had been popping up all over the city like whiteheads. And as a nightlife writer for the Boston Phoenix, it was my job to visit and write about them.

Now, I am fully aware that writing about lounges and clubs doesn't warrant much occupational bitching. Relatively speaking, I had a decent job, and looking back, I'm still surprised that it happened. My employment qualifications were not particularly impressive. I was five months out of university, I knew how to string sentences together, and I listened to four-on-the-floor club favorites like Underworld and Daft Punk on a daily basis. The prior candidate must have walked into the office with dog shit on their shoes, because one week after interviewing with the Phoenix editors, I got a phone call and an offer. But within a month of joining the paper, I learned a hard truth about modern nightlife journalism: modern journalism in general, really.

The problem was money. We didn't have any. And most of the industries and individuals I was tasked with covering were rolling in it.

So I settled into a strange double life—putting on a thrift store blazer, grabbing my notepad, and bumping shoulders with rich, beautiful Bostonians while fighting off thoughts about delinquent utility bills and what grocery stores sold the cheapest meat. The unseemliness of this binary existence was something I managed to ignore for the first eight months on the job. But when I arrived at the front door of Happy's on a sticky night in May and took a gander at the people inside, laughing, sipping Grey Goose and cranberry juice, exchanging business cards, I felt like running in the opposite direction. I didn't belong in there. My income bracket, social leverage, and small talk skills were no match for the Happy's crowd. This became even more apparent when I walked in, headed straight for the bar, and was cut off by two young men in suits with impeccably sculpted hair, having the following conversation.

"You know, I've never had one of these before!"

"What, a margarita served in a Mason jar?"

"Yeah! A margarita served in a Mason jar!"

"I think this is sea salt on the rim. It's really coarse."

"It's wicked coarse. It's gotta be sea salt!"

"I fuckin' *love* sea salt!"

This went on for about five minutes before a couple to my right vacated the bar, leaving an opening that I squeezed myself into as if it were a seat on a lifeboat. After handing over $8 for a bottle of Sam Adams, I wandered into the crowd and assumed a pose that I had come to calling "The Executive." This consisted of me wandering around, drink in one hand, phone in the other, intermittently scrolling through text messages and glancing up at the crowd, searching for some imaginary networking contact whom onlookers would (hopefully) assume I was there to meet. It might sound stupid, but it was preferable to looking as lost and uncomfortable as I felt. Unfortunately, the charade didn't last long because someone else at Happy's was looking for me.

"Miles!" I heard a voice shriek. I swiveled around, nearly sloshing beer all over Heather Curatone, the publicist who had arranged for me to attend the party. Heather represented nearly half of the nightlife venues I had visited and written about since joining the Phoenix. To cross her with an unflattering sentence about one of those venues was to risk being disinvited from events at all the other Heather Curatone-repped venues. Even for the Phoenix, arguably the last major publication in Boston with the temerity to ruffle well-fluffed feathers, being on Heather Curatone's shit list was a dangerous prospect. Much of the Phoenix's dwindling revenue came from local advertisements, including one-pagers for places like Happy's.

"Heather!" I exclaimed. "Love the new place!"

"Isn't it gorgeous?" she said. "You *have* to try the tiger shrimp and mango chutney sliders! There's a tray of them going around here somewhere."

"Tiger shrimp and mango chutney sliders?" I repeated. This was a move I had learned from nightlife networking. When in doubt, just feed the other person's lines back to them.

"Yeah!" Heather chimed. "Are you enjoying yourself?"

"You bet! All I need now is one of those sliders."

Heather turned to her right and shouted at a waitress who was doing her best to balance a tray on one hand while making her way through the crowd.

"Marcy! Front and center! I need you!"

"No, please, that's okay! I was just trying to be congenial," I interjected, but it was too late. The belabored waitress—Marcy, it would appear—headed straight for us with her tray, which contained five of the tiger shrimp and mango chutney sliders that Heather had spoken of so rapturously. They were nested in gold cupcake paper. Of course they were.

"I want to watch your reaction!" Heather said.

I grabbed a slider and pushed it into my mouth. Immediately, I knew that something was wrong: a pungent, acidic flavor profile that threatened to activate my gag reflex. *Grapefruit,* I realized with horror. *I fucking hate grapefruit.*

"Are you sure this is mango chutney?" I asked Heather through a mouthful of shrimp and fruit pulp.

"Oh my god! Is that what I said?" Heather laughed. "*Grapefruit* chutney. That's it! I hate mango!"

"So good," I managed to croak before swallowing a golf ball-sized mass. "I'll have to track down the recipe from the kitchen."

Heather turned on her heel with a smile and disappeared into the crowd. I watched her go and headed back to the bar to order another beer and recuperate.

I spent the rest of the evening at the bar, nursing my second Sam Adams, watching the bar staff juggle cocktail shakers and wine glasses. They were kids, barely older than me, and working like farm machinery. Watching them assemble drinks and swipe credit cards was exhausting, but at least at the bar, I could simply observe transactions taking place instead of participating in one. There was something desperate about the way that everyone in Happy's moved and talked. The bar staff performed their physical duties wordlessly and with urgency, as if being monitored by a choreographer who carried a riding crop around. There was a stench of vulnerability behind the bar, an odor that betrayed the aesthetic splendor of Happy's, and I suppose that's what kept me there until nearly 10 PM. It was starting to feel like a safe space.

A few days later, something happened that brought my own vulnerability to a head. All of the Phoenix staffers were summoned to a meeting with the publisher, Stephen Mindich. We made our way to the company boardroom, the one place in the building that had the ambience of a proper meeting space. (For perspective, all of the editorial desks were positioned under an open ceiling from which cables spilled like jungle vines.) Once the entire staff was packed into the room, Mindich, a squat guy with a ponytail and a mustache took a seat at the head of the table and announced, without much fanfare, that the Phoenix operating budget had reached a terminal point. Layoffs were coming. And they would happen across the board.

Most of the Phoenix staffers kept stone faced throughout the meeting. Hearing Mindich announce the beginning of the end must have felt like being slowly speared through the gut. Some of the staff had been working at the magazine for decades. They had kids and families to support. Just a week prior, I had overheard Justine, an editor who worked two desks away from me, talking on the phone, discussing a loved one's medical bills. After the meeting, most of us returned to our desks and silently resumed work. I noticed that Justine's desk was empty.

It was an unusually gusty afternoon for June, so I decided to walk home from work. I was still reeling from the bombshell that Mindich had just dropped on the Phoenix staff, and I didn't like the thought of being crammed in a fetid subway car with hundreds of misanthropic office workers trying to get home to enjoy a few precious hours of free time before waking up and doing it all over again. As I crossed the Boston University Bridge, feeling the sea breeze at my back, I heard the ring of a bicycle bell and turned around just in time to catch the cyclist grind to a halt.

It was Kelly Tomlin: a friend and former coworker whom I hadn't seen in years.

Some people don't believe that the universe orchestrates fateful meetings. Not me. I'm the sort of romantic who gets misty-eyed hearing stories about lovers who met for the first time at a restaurant when one began choking on a piece of boiled Sichuan fish and the other rushed over to perform the Heimlich maneuver. Maybe it's my way of rationalizing the comings and goings of a world that often makes no sense. Or perhaps I think this way because I've been the beneficiary of more than one fateful meeting. All I know is that as soon as Kelly Tomlin rang her bicycle bell, what happened next changed the course of my life.

Kelly was sweating from a brisk ride along the Charles, but it didn't matter. We hugged and spent a good 10 minutes or so sharing the respective details of our lives since...neither of us could recall the last time we had hung out. It must have been somewhere rugged. The two of us first met while working together in a network of wilderness hostels, deep in the White Mountains of New Hampshire. Our daily duties had included packing over 70 pounds of food and supplies up to the hostels on our backs. It was the sort of labor that allows you and another person to forge unfettered friendships, by breaking both of you down until you resemble wretched Gollum-like creatures. Since then, we had taken separate paths and lost touch. But meeting again, right there on the BU Bridge, we were shooting the shit as if those years hadn't elapsed. The details of Kelly's life that came out were intriguing. She had gotten a master's degree, and was waitressing in Somerville, looking for a teaching job with benefits and a viable future. The job hunt had been ongoing for quite some time, and her student loan payment notices were piling up at an alarming rate. Clearly, there was a lot to unpack here, so the two of us made plans to meet up the following week.

When our "date" arrived, I showed up at Kelly's duplex around sunset with a six-pack of lager. She had just gotten off her shift at the restaurant and was tired but ready to have a real conversation that didn't involve appeasing the other person. We sat in her kitchen with the windows open and drained the first two beers efficiently, commiserating about job prospects, debt, and our plans for the future, though "plans" seems like a generous word.

"I think a lot of us are living with the hope that things will just line up," Kelly said, opening her second beer and letting the cap skitter across the floor. "When I think of my parents as 20-somethings, I can imagine they had a solid idea of when they would own a house, have kids, that sort of thing. We don't have that."

"You mean, we don't have access to the same opportunities they did?" I said.

"Uh, fuck no. Remember the entry-level job? "

"Not really. But my mom could tell us some stories."

Kelly took a long swig of beer.

"I was at a high school reunion last month," she said. "And it was...like...there was this line between the people on a successful career track and the people on the 'I don't know what I'm doing' path."

"What do you hope your path looks like in the next five years?" I asked. "What would success look like to you?"

"I'd like to teach writing, reading, composition," Kelly said. "That's why I got my master's. But with the loan payments, on top of all the monthly bills...it's not like I can just put all my energy into job hunting and hold out for the right teaching job to open up. And that's the most frustrating part. I *want* to pay for my education. But it's very frustrating to be unable to use the knowledge I retained from school to pay for it."

There was a lull, during which I could hear crickets singing softly in the bushes outside.

"It's good to talk about these things," Kelly said. "I don't have health insurance, so, it's like...gotta keep the blood pressure at bay somehow!"

She laughed.

"But, I should say," Kelly turned to me with a more urgent look. "I don't want to come across as a whiny slacker. I've spent years trying to get some of these loans repaid. It just feels like the system we paid into is broken. You know?"

I nodded.

"Why do you think we're still paying into it?"

"I'm guessing a lot of people are still very afraid of being thought of as anything less than a classic "American" who pulls themselves up by their bootstraps when things get tough."

"Right," I agreed. "We're only as good as our hard work. Pain and anguish are the only means of purification. It's the inner Calvinist in all of us. Or inner Protestant? I can never remember."

"I think we should start flogging people," Kelly said. "Bring that back."

"Or the stocks," I said. "Let people pelt student debtors with expired vegetables. I don't know about you, but I'd take a faceful of rancid cabbage over a date with the bankruptcy court."

"It's just so stupid!" Kelly exclaimed. "This whole game we're playing with loans has changed! And people are still holding themselves to the old standards. It's like watching two guys try to play checkers after the checkerboard has suddenly disappeared. You wanna tap one of them on the shoulder and be like, 'Um...what the fuck are you doing buddy?'"

The two of us killed the rest of the beer. It was after midnight when I said goodnight to Kelly and began the half-drunken walk back to Central Square, the neighborhood of Cambridge I had been living in. For such a bleak conversation, the effect on my mind had been rejuvenating. I felt unencumbered—like someone had taken a great weight off my shoulders. I could have spent the rest of the night talking with Kelly about the less-than-robust economy that our generation had inherited. I was no stranger to the worried conversations about student loans and unemployment. I had debts of my own to pay, and my job at the Phoenix would likely be gone within the year. But during the months prior to hanging out with Kelly, my mind had been preoccupied with the logistical and social demands of working:

of being a young professional.[1] The more substantive issues involving young adults had been blips on my radar.

As I would learn in the coming weeks, through research conducted during my lunch hour and into the small hours of the night, those issues were hardly blips.

In 2012, nearly 17% of young American adults were unemployed. And that figure doesn't even include young adults who had given up looking for work. Among these young adults, the average student debt estimate was $26,500. Academics and pundits were already presenting these statistics as markers of a profoundly fucked generation. "Millennial," a term coined by historians Neil Howe and William Strauss, was the word chosen to classify this unlucky class of young Americans, born between 1982 and 2002. For such a sexy word, being called "Millennials" felt more like a badge of shame. And it didn't help that much of the Baby Boomer cognoscenti had begun the generational tradition of denigrating their offspring as insipid little twats with no respect for what their elders had suffered through. Don't like your job? *Just be grateful you have a job, you entitled crybaby.* Can't find a job? *The world owes you nothing—grow up!* Sinking into student loan debt?

---

[1] "Young professional" is a term used to describe a 20-something adult with career prospects in the white-collar sector. It's mostly used by Millennials who are applying for apartments.

That's your fault. No one forced you to get a degree. I think Clint Eastwood put it best back in the summer of 2016, sagely observing, "We're really in a pussy generation right now."

It was hardly a unique frustration, weathering contempt from the old guards. But after too many nights of lying awake, staring out my window at the one street light in sight and listening to the wind shaking the leaves, wondering if I would ever be able to support a family or even own a house one day, I became fed up of being called names by adults who had enjoyed better employment prospects and compensation standards. The Millennial jabs made me angrier than they should have. I didn't know many Millennials who lived up to such an unflattering stereotype. Most of them were working too hard to afford the luxury of being a lousy employee or human being. And so, one day, it occurred to me that a useful thing to do would be to talk to some of those Millennials—just as I had talked with Kelly. Only this time, I would record the conversations, transcribe them, and share them with any audience willing to consider the experiences and perspectives of young adults. And each conversation would boil down to one central question.

What do you care about?

If debt and underemployment were the issues that kept Kelly and I up at night, what were the other roots of Millennial insomnia, and how deep did they run?

A plan came into focus. I would quit the
Phoenix before my job ended up on the fiscal
chopping block. I would sustain myself with a
variety of seasonal labor jobs and whatever
freelance writing assignments I could get my
hands on. That would leave roughly three or four
months of the year during which I could sublease
my room and travel around America, searching
for Millennials who were willing to talk about their
lives, their hopes, and their anxieties. I didn't know
what form these interviews would eventually take.
A book? A series of articles? A YouTube channel?
All I knew was that jotting down the testimonies of
Generation Screwed, as an addendum to U.S.
history, seemed like a more valuable use of my
time and energy than writing about the virtues of
recessed lighting in lounges, or hotshot chefs who
cooked exclusively with duck fat. It would be a
thrill, and yes, a privilege, to apply the interview
skills I had developed as a nightlife journalist to a
project with more humanist substance.

After writing my letter of resignation and
handing it in on the same day that my editor
announced his imminent departure from the
Phoenix, I spent the fall and winter bussing tables,
recording snowfall and shoveling shit deep in in
the New Hampshire woods, writing marketing
copy for a college admissions department and a
Jewish prep school blog, and selling my body to
researchers at McLean and Massachusetts General

21

Hospital. ("No drugs, radiation, or catheters" was my golden rule when volunteering as a paid guinea pig for medical studies.) By the following spring, I had amassed a nest egg and purchased a sheath of Greyhound bus tickets for my first Millennial interviews tour. The trip took me from the Maine woods to the beaches of Marina Del Rey. I slept on couches, carpets, and in at least two bathtubs. I spoke with exactly 73 young adults over the course of the summer. Between the years 2013 and 2016, three additional Millennial tours followed—my favorite involved traveling nearly 200 miles on foot, in the middle of winter. Most of the Millennials I interviewed were encountered at random on public transportation, college campuses, or in restaurants, stores, and other workplaces. I was surprised by how many of these young adults consented to be interviewed, often with no hesitation. Some of them introduced me to friends of theirs. Some of them are now friends of mine.

There was just one problem. Throughout this years-long project, as the Millennial interview recordings piled up into the hundreds, filling multiple hard drives, I couldn't decide what to do with the transcripts. I tried fashioning the first wave of interviews into a travel memoir, only to put the unfinished draft on mothballs out of creative frustration. I pitched articles to new outlets, but the only one that landed was two page rebuttal to an NPR contributor's lambasting of parents who allowed their Millennial-aged children to live at home—it was more of an editorial pissing contest than a revelatory exchange about the Millennial experience. A chill of doubt crept in. Was my Millennials project an inherently narcissistic endeavor? After all, who was I to think anyone would care about hearing what my generation had to say about life, work, and the future?

What kept me going was a little vibration that ran through me immediately after every Millennial interview I conducted. If I had to compare this sensation to something more tangible, I would ask you to imagine being seated in a dinghy, balanced atop a massive wave in the ocean. I didn't know what the wave signified, but I could feel it getting bigger beneath me.

Like all waves, it would eventually crash down and reshape everything.

THE EARTHQUAKE

On April 25, 2016—roughly three years after I started interviewing Millennials— the U.S. Census Bureau quietly released a population report with seismic implications for America. After decades of the Baby Boomers dominating election cycles, the ground had finally shifted. But it wasn't Generation X that outgrew the Boomers—it was the Millennials. Overnight, my peers and I had become the largest living generation in America.

Barely anyone noticed.

At this particular moment, most eyes in America were fixated on another event that would have similarly game-changing consequences. The 2016 U.S. presidential election was flaring up into an inferno that exceeded the cable news punditry's most torrid fantasies. What many had predicted would be a dull contest between former Secretary of State Hillary Clinton and former Governor of Florida Jeb Bush (Jeb!) became a months-long cage fight that pitted politics as usual against an emergent American populism that manifested itself in two *very* different figures.

On the left, Independent Vermont Senator Bernie Sanders challenged the Democratic Party's recent history of embracing centrist policy—he called for bolder solutions to problems like wealth inequality, global warming, and campaign finance laws that opened the floodgates to money from corporations and comically wealthy donors like Sheldon Adelson and the Mercer family. The Sanders insurgency launched on the banks of Lake Champlain with a modest crowd in attendance, but it swelled into a stadium-filling, small donation-fueled juggernaut that came close to derailing the Clinton campaign. Judging from the total amount of money raised by the grassroots campaign—more than $228 million—a *lot* of people connected with Bernie's keynote message that the U.S. government was no longer working in the interest of ordinary American people, and that a "political revolution" was the only way to restore fairness and opportunity to the American landscape. Even when Hillary Clinton eventually won the Democratic nomination, it was clear that Sanders had claimed a bigger prize—the incendiary will of those who felt marginalized and untrusting of the Capitol Hill class.

But not all of the disenfranchised were feeling the Bern. From the Republican primary, which began with *17 candidates* locking horns for the presidential ticket, an unlikely victor emerged. Donald Trump, the real estate mogul and former reality TV star, a man whom many assumed was running for president as a publicity stunt, quickly amassed an enthusiastic following of American voters. Leveraging the sentiment that fueled Bernie's run—the notion that America's "elites" had lost touch with the concerns of ordinary people—Trump promised a more austere and nativist set of solutions. These included deporting millions of undocumented immigrants and building a giant wall across America's southern border, punishing U.S. companies that outsourced jobs to countries with cheaper labor, and funneling vast amounts of money into the police and military budgets to combat perceived threats from without and within. Compared to his rivals—even within the Republican Party—Trump offered a dark and largely unsubstantiated vision of America and the world[2], but it was a vision that resonated strongly with voters whose futures had been eroding before their eyes for decades.

Having spent three years listening to young adults express many of the same frustrations that transformed a self-described Democratic Socialist and a self-described sexual predator[3] into political heavyweights, I had one dominant thought while watching the rise of Bernie Sanders and Donald Trump. *This was the wave!* The anxieties and dreams of my generation—plus the mutual resentments between Millennials and Baby Boomers—had yielded two angry movements against America's political establishment. The Millennials overwhelmingly embraced Bernie's vision of more Scandinavian version of America while Boomers boarded the Trump train. This was the beginning of something huge, historic, and surprising only for its delayed onset. Most of the symptoms had been glaringly visible in the cities, suburbs, and stretches of countryside I had visited during my Millennial research. The distinguishing features of America, as I saw it, were the derelict homes, the shuttered businesses, the exorbitant

---

[2] On the campaign trail, Trump described America's cities as crime-ridden hellholes and characterized immigrants and refugees from Muslim nations as likely terrorists. Both assertions are resoundingly dispelled by statistics, but this did not dissuade Trump from reasserting both claims.

[3] A leaked audio recording from "Access Hollywood," which surfaced shortly before the 2016 election, features Trump admitting to grabbing women "by the pussy" and kissing them without their consent.

price tags one encountered in any place where there were still jobs to be found, and most of all, the sunken faces and uncertain voices of the young people I met and spoke with.

By autumn, as Clinton and Trump engaged in their first televised debate, it dawned on me that these young people, now the largest generation in America, could determine the outcome of the 2016 election. We had the numbers to push the electoral needle left or right. It wasn't just a question of which candidate most Millennials would vote for, but whether most Millennials would bother to vote at all. Our participation in the 2014 midterms—a dismal 21.3%—suggested that most of us might stay home again on November 8th. But Millennials also played an important role in boosting Barack Obama to victory twice[4], and those elections took place before most Millennials were old enough to vote.

This presented the Democrats and Republicans with two roads to victory. The first was logical and simple: reach out to Millennials and inspire them to believe in the efficacy of voting by offering reasonable solutions to their reasonable concerns about America and the future. The second road was the mother of all political gambles: pray that the other party would fail to engage Millennials, throw some red meat to the most anxiety-ridden Baby Boomers, and then benefit from the

---

[4] In the 2008 and 2012 elections, more than 60% of the young adults who voted chose Obama.

mediocre youth turnout on Election Day.

The Democrats took neither of these two roads, focusing instead on Trump's temperament and lack of political experience,[5] which amounted to a campaign pitch of "I'm not with stupid."

The Republicans chose the second road.

On November 8, 2016, Donald Trump became the 44th President of the United States of America.

THE UNANSWERED QUESTION

When the exit polls were published, they revealed that roughly 50% of eligible Americans had voted in the 2016 election. That is *staggeringly* low participation rate, and the same breakdown can be applied to Millennial voting. The Millennials who filled out ballots by November 8th amounted to slightly less than half of all Millennials who were old enough to vote. Most of them chose Clinton over Trump, but evidently, these votes were not cast with the sort of enthusiasm that prompts young people to drag their friends to the local polling place on Election Day. Most of the surveys proctored to Millennial voters before the election came back with the same conclusion—Millennials were not thrilled

---

[5] A 2017 study from the Wesleyan Media Project revealed that only 25% of the Clinton campaign's advertisements highlighted the Democratic Party platform. Most of the ads—which cost $172 million total—went after Trump and spotlighted his lack of qualifications for being president.

about their options. In fact, a UMass Lowell and Odyssey poll found that 1 in 4 Millennials would have preferred a giant meteor colliding with the Earth over voting for either Clinton or Trump. I swear, I'm not making this up.

We have now witnessed what can happen to America when Millennials use less than their full political power as the largest living generation. The wave that will now reshape America was directed by the concerns of an elder generation that compensated for its dwindling numbers by besting the youth at voting. (Sorry, liberal boomers, but the exit data doesn't lie.) This generational usurpation of political capital had immediate consequences. Following Trump's victory, global stock markets tanked and soared within a handful of weeks. Diplomatic relations between the U.S. and ally nations such as Mexico, Germany, and Australia soured in just as little time. On January 20, the day that Trump was officially sworn into office, all references to "climate change" mysteriously vanished from the White House website. The next day, millions of people in more than 60 countries participated in a series of women's marches that spanned all seven continents. Domestically, it was the largest day of protests in U.S. History.

Are Millennials somehow responsible for all of this? Would Hillary Clinton be in the White House today if Millennials had voted *en masse*? Would the world feel less vulnerable to upheaval by angry mobs? More than a few people have posed these questions—mostly Democrats and almost always through gritted teeth. But in this writer's opinion, these are the wrong questions to be asking, in light of such surprising and consequential political developments. Instead of mourning what could have happened in this past race, it's now time to address the unanswered question that will loom large over the next election cycle.

What do Millennials believe in?

The answer to this question is exactly what I spent three years searching for, across America. The answers are an intel well that could transform a disempowered political organization—not just the Democratic Party, but an emergent third party—into a force to be reckoned with in future races. But more importantly, the answers to this question allow us a glimpse at what America could look like when Millennials unleash their full voting power and begin to assume roles in public office. The passage of time and the finite lifespan of the species guarantee both of these turning points, just as they assure all young people that one day, they will call the shots.

And so, in the interest of further cracking open the nutshell of Millennials, what they want, and how they plan to fight for it, I have decided to release this book.

What you are about to read is a handpicked

selection of the Millennial interviews that I conducted during the years of 2013 through 2016—starting at the height of Barack Obama's presidency and concluding on the eve of Donald Trump's electoral upset. The interviews here were chosen from hundreds to offer a proportional representation of the viewpoints I encountered during my travels and research. All names have been changed to protect the identities of the featured Millennials, but the stories and ideas expressed here are the ones that stayed with me long after I hung up my backpack and transcribed my interview recordings. If I have done my job properly, some of the thoughts expressed in these interviews will leave you grinning with hope, while others will make you consider buying a machine gun or immigrating to Cape Breton. (According to Justin Trudeau, the latchstring is always out.) But for anyone wondering how the hell America moves forward from the partisan dogma and toxicity of the 2016 election cycle, the following pages are a fine place at which to start. They comprise nothing less than an introduction to America's newest generation of constituents, activists, pundits, lobbyists, legislators, and yes, presidents.

Reader, I'd like you to meet **The Early Voters**.

"No one expected me.
Everything awaited me."

Patti Smith
Just Kids, 2010

MADDY

23 years old
Mentoring Assistant
Farmington, New Mexico

February 23, 2013

INTERIOR. A small kitchen. Some potted succulents. Lots of natural light spilling in from outside. It's late winter.

Let's start with what you're doing right now. What does a sketch of your current life look like?

Well, at the moment, I coordinate after school mentoring programs for kids in the 6-18 age range, which is something I've never done before! It's a pretty exciting learning experience for me. I'm overseeing about 280 kids, each of whom get paired with multidisciplinary mentors at the club I work at for one-on-one meetings, once a week. Basically, I need to make sure that grants are fulfilled, that our donors are recognized, and that mentors are paired with the right kids each week. I'm also working to design and build a community garden at the club. I met up with a landscape architect who works for the city of Santa Fe, who's been eying this empty lot near my workplace. We've drawn up a design and budget already, so now it's being circulated for approval by the club president and directors. Even if we can't build a community garden, we're going to have gardening be an aspect of the summer programming. We can at least get a few pots of tomatoes going and I can build a curriculum around gardening and nutrition.

Sounds like the agrarian childhood many of us wish we had.

It's so fulfilling to be able to put ideas that you have into action. To be in a position where I can propose ideas like, "What if I brought the kids on a field trip to look at a college greenhouse," and actually make them happen!

And has the Farmington area always been home for you?

No, I grew up in New Jersey. And honestly, moving west was like a dream come true. At 17, I'd become very frustrated with my high school classmates, my parents, and I was bored: I remember fantasizing about going somewhere else. So one day, I actually decided to do it. I found a college I could afford to go to, told my teachers I wanted to graduate, and to me, it was like revenge on everything I'd been angry about. It felt like the biggest adventure. I went from living in my parents' house one week and suddenly, the next week, I was in another part of the country, going to parties, getting to meet all kind of students, stay out until 4 AM, and studying Ancient Greek, which nobody I knew around home had done.

But Ancient Greek wasn't your only focus.

Well, when I first went to college I'd actually been sure I wanted to study writing. That was how I presented myself. As a writer. People thought of me as a writer: friends, parents. But I decided to study liberal arts instead, and it was because I thought *that* would make me a better writer. To have a creative life first.

Now, fast-forward three years ahead, to graduation.
How were you feeling about your decision?

The funny thing is, when I started senior year, I
became overwhelmed by the thought of
graduation, and getting a full-time "real" job. I'd
spent the summer working at the Georgia O'Keeffe
museum doing art education instruction, keeping
with the whole creative life idea. But one day, I
found this journal I'd been writing during my first
weeks of college. Typical girl thing to do. I'd
sketched out a projected timeline of my life from
2008 to 2011. And within it, I'd written, *"I'm gonna*
go to the Peace Corps after I graduate." At first, it
seemed like a joke to me but the more I thought
about it, I realized this felt like the perfect plan! I
felt it was exactly what I was meant to do. I wanted
to do an agricultural assignment in Africa, learn
traditional farming techniques, and to write about
it while I was there. Then come back and work for
the USDA. So I applied, and the Peace Corps
accepted me. I packed up, and moved to Brooklyn
to stay with a friend for the interim. Just to have
some fun while I was waiting for my deployment.
But then, I started having severe pain in my feet.
Very suddenly. It got worse.

Without any warning? Were you able to walk?

Barely. To put a long story into a few words, I had
several tests done by a bunch of doctors, and I was

given two pieces of very bad news, in a matter of weeks. I'd developed rheumatoid arthritis, and I also had thyroid cancer. "Also."

Jesus. To get those diagnoses in such a short period of time-

It was hell. It was *extremely* hard. It's been almost year since my thyroid surgery and I was thinking this week about how I've done so much since then and hardly had a minute to rest. I don't think it's something I've completely come to terms with. I mean, when I got diagnosed with cancer, I already felt so shell-shocked over the arthritis. I wasn't even that surprised. The attitude I had was, "*Of course I fucking have cancer.*" Things were so bad they seemed laughable. I told an ex-boyfriend recently that during that period of time, I felt like I was walking on top of a black hole.

How did these terrible developments alter your life initially?

I felt like I had no stability anymore. My body was unwell, I had no job, barely any money, and because of my illness and doctors, I had to remain close to New York City, which was never the plan or something I had budgeted for. I had no stable place to live, my relationships in life got rocky, and I tried new diets, medications that messed up my immune system. I remember: my concept of self was *completely* shattered. I had no idea what would happen in the future.

How did you hold your life together, with so much uncertainty and pain in your waking existence?

In college, some friends of mine had been studying eastern philosophy. My boyfriend was translating Sanskrit. And I'd gone to the college Zen center and meditated before, which introduced me to Buddhism. Though I wouldn't have called myself a Buddhist by any means. But on New Year's Day 2012, in New York, I decided to go to a Buddhist ceremony in the morning, meditating and offering incense, a vow for compassion. Later that day, my dad and younger brother came into Brooklyn to help me move out of my friend's living room to a more permanent place I'd found in Washington Heights, near Harlem. One of Dad's closest friends since he was young—Barry—is a Buddhist who happened to live in Washington Heights. And that day, I found out that Barry was hosting a *Toso*.

A Toso?

It's a chant that lasts at least one hour. And this came as such a coincidence. I wasn't able to make it to Barry's Toso, but after I finished moving, my dad, brother and I all went to the after-party: a whole bunch of Buddhists hanging out after *four hours* of chanting. I'm a naturally inquisitive person, so I talked to the people there about chanting. Within weeks, I was chanting every day. Singing too. It didn't spring from a rational place, or help me draw deep conclusions about the universe, but it felt good.

I can imagine. I think a lot of people would like the sound of chanting. Just "letting it all out" for an hour each day.

The great thing about this form of Buddhism is that you can chant with other people *or* by yourself. Anytime during the day. And it's not formal, so you don't have to stress about dress, posture, breathing, etc. My first time, I went home to my apartment, I was sitting on my bed, and I just said *"I'm gonna chant now."* It was freeing, exhilarating, I felt like I wanted to laugh.
With chanting, you can be whoever you are, wherever you are, and put your heart into chant. I knew I needed to open up my own heart and I wanted spiritual practice that wasn't coming from any sense of obligation or fear. My mother's family is Jewish, and I've done some Jewish forms of praying, but in those moments, I'd often think, *"Am I doing this right? Pronouncing this properly like the Rabbi told me?"* Now I can have spirituality that isn't given to me by anyone else.

You mentioned that you would sing too. Was this something you engaged in prior to your diagnosis?

Not for years. So strange, and right after my thyroid surgery too. I mean, my voice was hoarse, and I had scars all over my throat, but this was another thing that didn't come rationally. I thought, "*I used to do this all the time as a kid, so why don't I do it anymore?*" At the time, my boyfriend was teaching himself to play guitar, and he'd sometimes play for me. So I sang. The initial experience was painful and mortifying because I wanted to sing for him but I sounded so awkward, having not practiced for ages. But I realized the desire was still there. I'd left that part of me diminished. I went out, and I bought a ukulele. I needed the instrument to sing for me. Keep in mind, I was still broke and could barely afford most things after rent, and the ukulele was a cheap instrument. I didn't even buy a case or tuner. After the surgery I was tired, and working as a tutor in the evening. So when I wasn't going out with friends, I'd sit around the apartment and teach myself to play.

What happened when the day of reckoning arrived? When you eventually had to find a more substantial job to support yourself.

That was a big drama. By April last year, I was seeing my doctors less often. A part of me wanted to stay in New York because I have friends there but I didn't know how I'd be able to pay my rent. So I sat down and thought, "*Alright, I need a job, a place to live, but also, a place to heal.*" I recalled that my young cousins had attended this very respected summer camp for girls in upstate New York, and I decided to apply for job there. And sure enough, I was hired to be a camping instructor, which I was thrilled about! I loved camping during college and I'd soon be leading 12 year-old girls on overnight trips. How awesome is that? The problem was, I needed my doctor to sign a form saying I was healthy enough to take the job and he wouldn't sign it. He said, "*You can't be hiking!*" I actually broke down in his office, and started crying because I felt panicked, like this needed to happen. If I couldn't get out of NYC and take this job, I wouldn't have a place to live. And my doctor just wanted to put me on antidepressants because I started crying in his office.

How did you find a way to circumvent such a frustrating situation?

Well, I was able to hold it together, and I just told the camp director the whole matter. And she offered me a different job. First, I was supposed to be head of the canoeing department, which was funny because I don't know a thing about canoeing. When I actually got to the camp, I was switched to farm and gardening. It turned out to be the best thing I could have done.

Sounds pretty labor intensive though. How demanding was your new life as a counselor?

It was a 24-hour job. We lived in Boy Scout style tents. Myself and three girls. I was their mom for eight weeks. I slept in the tent with them, and there was no privacy. We couldn't have the flaps of our tent down. Had to keep them up at all times.

From the second I woke up, I made sure the girls were awake and dressed. I served them food and cleaned their plates at breakfast. The girls weren't allowed to serve themselves. And the whole time, I'd make conversation, funny jokes, and ask questions. We'd return to the tent, I'd have the girls clean up their spaces and then we'd plan our day. The camp was built on a philosophy where the girls
choose what they want to do each day.

You mean the campers get to design the whole curriculum?

Well, the counselors help them make the best choices to feel most positive about themselves, as in *"Oh, I noticed you tried water skiing yesterday and it didn't work out for you, but don't you think it might be fun to try it again?"* But I'd spend a portion of each day with the girls working in the farm and garden. We'd be milking goats, taking care of pigs, chickens, making cheese, planting vegetables, and tackling barn tasks. And by the time we were done, the day would only be half-over! With a 9 PM bedtime, we were always working.

Looking ahead, in the next five to ten years, what do you hope to be doing with your life?

I really want to be able to control my arthritis without taking medication. I don't know whether or not I can do that, because serious drugs that are commonly used to treat the symptoms tend to mess with your body and immune system. So I'm trying to stay healthy in other ways. I watched documentary about Chuck Close[1] recently and I felt like I need to think about making art again, in the near future.

You might recall from our phone chat that all of these interviews I'm conducting are an attempt to unpack the word "Millennial." Drawing from your own experiences and those of your peers, reflecting and looking ahead, how do you identify with the label "Millennial?"

I'm only 22 years old, and I don't think I can really formulate a specific statement, but I mean...I'm scared about the future. I'm lucky to have health insurance at least. I met someone in Maine who lives in my mom's hospice who's now 27 and when he was 21, he got testicular cancer. Now he's thousands of dollars in debt.

Your mom is in hospice care at the moment?

My mom got was diagnosed with stage 4 lung cancer a few weeks after I moved to New Mexico. I had just finished building this Buddhist altar I'd been meaning to assemble for months. It's in my room now, and I chant to it. Think of it as a mirror of my own life, something that I guard: a very profound thing. The day after I built my altar, my mom was admitted to ER, as the cancer had spread to her brain. It's bizarre...it's like...I'm

---

[1] Chuck Close is best known for his abstract paintings, many of which are enormous in scale.

still trying to figure out why these are the cards that are being dealt to me. I don't understand.

How do you stay connected with your mom, in the wake of this news?

I write a lot of letters to her. I struggled to know what to do at first, because she's so far away. Now we talk on the phone every day. She does have some memory problems, in the short-term, so it can be disturbing for me. Her letters are a way for her to know that I'm thinking of her, and I realized this made me feel better. I write to a lot of other friends too. And on the side, I've finally started taking ukulele lessons. This morning, my teacher and I decided to work on "After Hours" by The Velvet Underground.

You mentioned health insurance as one of your greatest concerns. That alone paints a grave picture of our healthcare system and the burden it can place upon families dealing with cancer and other debilitating diseases.

I'm in a fortunate place, to be covered. Where I'm at now, I get my salary from the government, and while it's set at the poverty level, I get insurance, and an education stipend at the end of the year if I finish my assignment.

Is that something you're concerned about right now? Making a salary that hovers right around the poverty level?

I know I'm not making much money and I definitely feel an enormous amount of pressure. My grandfather has been sending me emails saying, *You need to figure out how to make 200K a year so you can take care of yourself and have something left over for charity*. Pressuring me on how to get back into school, saying I should study biology, that sort of thing. And yes, I've only been in my current job for three months. But where was I six months ago? A year ago? I've come so far.

NAT

27 years old
Food Truck Owner
Oakland, California

June 14, 2013

INTERIOR. An industrial kitchen. Steel appliances. The aroma of griddled onions. Someone is pulling a navy tray from the oven.

So how exactly does one wake up one morning and say, "Fuck it, I'm gonna open my own food truck."

You know, I'm still not sure. Before I moved out here from the east coast, I had some kitchen experience working in a chain of family restaurants. When I got to Oakland, one of my first jobs involved cooking on another food truck and also at this cafe that was very poorly run but still doing decent business. It was one of those moments where I thought, "Jeez, *I* could do this." And eventually, the idea for my own truck—a gourmet Midwestern hamburger truck—it just came to me, really. I had wanted to start my own business for a while, and I was still young enough to not know any better. So I figured I might as well give it shot while I didn't have any dependents.

What was it about food trucks in particular that interested you? As opposed to, say, a more traditional restaurant?

The food truck craze was really catching on in the Bay Area right around this time. And from my insight to the restaurant industry, it seemed like starting a truck would be a lot more economically attainable and sustainable than a building up a brick and mortar business.

Tell me about your cooking method. How did you develop your Midwestern burger recipe? What makes it unique!

Each summer, I used to drive from New Jersey to California. And I had this restaurant book called *Roadfood* with me, by Jane and Michael Stern. They recommended a burger shack in Salina, Kansas called The Cozy Inn. So I went there and they served the best cheeseburgers I've ever had. In the backroom, you could see cooks shoving onions into a food processor and then blending them with ground beef. That was it, other than a little salt and pepper. They'd make these balls of burger meat, and then literally smash them onto the griddle and reshape them. It gives the burger this great, flavorful char without overcooking the meat inside. Basically, this way of cooking was adopted for creating the burger that we now serve on the truck. And we use an old-fashioned clothing iron to do the smashing.

Cool, so you had a tangible, edible dream. How did you begin to go about realizing it?

First, I had to get to the point of admitting to myself that I was actually going to do this. It took about seven months of moping around. I finally tried saying it out loud to somebody and it was that situation where you're worried they'll be like, "Start a food truck? That's fucking stupid."

Did you have to weather much skepticism when you

started sharing the idea?

Actually, not much! It was almost the opposite outcome, where I told someone about the idea and they'd say, "Oh, you should totally do that." Then you gain more confidence, and your pitch evolves into, "I'm writing a *business plan* for a food truck."

What was your business plan? Had you ever done anything like this before?

No, not at all. It was extremely different from anything I'd put together before. I started my research by calling people who ran other food trucks, hoping to get some concrete budget numbers and sales projections etched out before I sunk any money into the truck. And that alone was very difficult: getting other people involved in the industry to talk to me. Especially since I wasn't in the business yet. In fact, now that I'm in the business, I can definitely understand how easy it would be to lose track of some unknown voicemail to the effect of, "Hey. I'm interested in starting a food truck. Do you have half an hour so I can pick your brain?"

Did your initial research boost or shake your confidence?

What I learned quickly was that food trucks are a bleeding edge industry. And a lot of them still don't understand their own sales projections, profit margins, or even how much money they invested to get their truck up and running. Not to mention, how much money they have squirreled away, just in case.

And how much money did it take to start the truck?

Well, the truck itself was easy to figure out. I just went to a truck dealership, essentially, and found that a refurbished, middle-of-the-road food truck would cost me $35,000. Then, from there, let's see...the wrap[1] would cost another $4,000. And then you need a professional kitchen to prepare the food in each morning, before loading up the truck. So you have to factor in rent prices as well. I assumed these would be the bulk of expenses to get the truck going. I ended up taking out a loan to pay for the truck itself and I paid for the wrap with my savings.

Did this give you the momentum to start planning your truck?

Basically. From that point, writing the business plan was almost like anthropology. Most people don't speak the food truck language, there's no scientific research being done on them, and there's very little to compare your plan to. A lot of it is guesswork. So I just went about projecting sales, costs, wages, and profits, most of which were based on a completely unrealistic work-life balance. [laughs] Originally, the truck team wasn't going to be working too much, which is definitely not the case now!

---

[1] The "wrap" is a giant decal that covers a food truck and makes it appear illustrated.

How many hours do you put in per week, on average?

These days, I could be looking at 60 hours, but I usually put in about 50 and say, "Good enough."

What kind of food licenses did you have to acquire in order to legally sell burgers?

All kinds! You've got to incorporate your business. We're an LLC.[2] To this day, I still have a pretty vague understanding of what that means. Each license almost always requires something else. You need an LLC to get a seller's permit, which you need in order to apply for a health permit. The state of California is pretty cash strapped, and for a while, getting these documents from them was like extortion.

So the fees were exorbitant?

The fees are *still* exorbitant. I think California has actually been ranked the number one worst American state to do business in.[3] They just ding you everywhere they can. The Board of Equalization, which collects sales tax, requires a

---

[2] LLC is an acronym for "Limited Liability Company." In other words, a small business.

[3] Nat is correct. In 2015, the annual ChiefExecutive.net survey—which includes input from more than 500 U.S. CEOs—named California the worst state to do business in, for the eleventh consecutive year. The state's tax codes and regulatory standards were cited as cumbersome for business owners.

$2,000 deposit in order to do business in California. They claim it's just in case you can't pay your own sales tax. But still...the idea of taking $2,000 from the cash flow of a brand new business because the state can't afford to pay its own taxes still strikes me as bullshit. And then there's the inefficiencies at state level. We literally had to drive to Sacramento to ask for our incorporation papers to be returned! Because we needed them to secure the loan that would cover most of the truck's startup costs. But now, the truck is finally starting to pay for itself.

After the truck opened, how long did it take to get to a point where you were coming out even, financially?

The truck stopped being a money sink after about two years. I'm no longer so sure that food trucks are that much cheaper than small restaurants!

Okay, so...opening day. How had you been getting word about the truck out there? What were the inaugural crowds like? Were there crowds?

We hadn't done much outreach other than telling our friends about the truck. We had an opening party in our driveway, which was pretty well attended and got us some more starter cash. Our first day serving to the public felt crazy. We didn't know what we were doing at all, and the work was very stressful. The opening weeks were a learning process.

How often do you spend time thinking about the long-term future of the truck, as opposed to...say...the next month?

Less and less, really. The truck is old and we often have pieces of machinery breaking down, or unforeseen labor shortages. As a business owner, it makes sense to be thinking extensively about the big picture, but the fact is, the business is still growing. And with that growth, we've made mistakes. Part of my role is to ensure damage control and make sure that we learn from each mistake.

What challenges do you imagine yourself facing in the next five to ten years?

The truck is a fairly viable business operation and right now, I can support my lifestyle with it. But it's going to have to grow substantially if I'm going to support myself plus any dependents that might come along down the road. One of our more successful ventures lately has been breaking into catering. We've done a bunch of weddings and even some high-end corporate gigs. We did one for Facebook last week. It was a real victory for us.

Jeez. Complimentary Midwestern smash burgers? The perks of working in Silicon Valley truly know no limits.

Oh, and not just burgers. We tend to roll out specialty menus for the catering jobs. All with local ingredients. For Facebook, we served smoked macaroni and cheese, pulled pork sliders, blueberry cobbler...it takes a lot of planning and time, but it's worth the effort.

I'm in the wrong trade.

It's pretty surreal. [laughs] Being surrounded by all that wealth, bringing out food. It's an interesting dynamic.

But, like Zuck,[4] you've succeeded as an entrepreneur. The truck might not have the backing of venture capitalists, but it's not a money sink and it sounds like you've got some loyal customers. How do you think your situation compares to that of other Millennials these days?

I think about that a lot, actually. It's hard not to. The whole evisceration of the middle class seems pretty real to me. Especially here in the Bay Area. You've got a lot of jobs going to these extremely well trained professionals in tech who get paid a ton of money, and that's one of the things that drives up the rent and cost of living for everyone else. People like you or me. I mean, it's classic gentrification, but right here, it's happening at a rate I've never even heard of before. Not even what happened in Brooklyn just a few years ago.

Has your rent gone up lately?

----

[4] This is the improbably chummy way in which people often refer to Mark Zuckerberg around the Bay Area. It's infectious. It makes you sound cool.

Yeah. It's a borderline crisis if you live across the bay, in the city. But the thing is, you can't think about these issues *too* much. Especially if you're already working around the clock to put food on the table or keep a roof over your head. And that's something I worry about, with our generation. I worry about consciousness. Obviously, Millennials are very aware of all these driving social and environmental issues—gay marriage, clean energy, organic food—and that's great. But it's hard to move beyond just caring if you're struggling to support yourself.

Except, you could argue that if it gets even harder for more and more Millennials to find jobs that will pay enough to buy groceries and living space, that could push them into action as well: the desperation.

Maybe. It could. I definitely don't think our generation is lazy. Most Millennials I know are hard workers. It's just like most people would act, when thrown in a big pool. You've gotta swim to survive. I don't know too many people who spend their days watching YouTube videos.

Me neither, but do you think there's anything different about the way we approach work? Right or wrong, we're not exactly the toast of the American office.

I think there's a fixation on working smarter. Like, using tools we have available to do our jobs more effectively and live healthier, more balanced lives.

In exchange, it seems like Millennials are settling for not having as much disposable income as our parents did. It's definitely not the first thing on my list of concerns. A lot of us grew up in a bubble that's no longer there, and I see a lot of people my age...well, anyone who's not making hand-over-fist in the tech sector...I see a lot of Millennials accepting or even embracing the idea that our lives will probably be more modest than our what our parents had.

PRIYA

24 years old
Research Assistant
Washington, D.C.

March 8, 2013

EXTERIOR. A grassy common surrounded by tall buildings. People in business formal attire are milling around. Some are eating lunch in the sun.

It's not every day that you meet someone involved in national security policy research, especially at a place as esteemed as Brookings Institute. What does your average workday look like?

Being a research assistant means many different things, depending on whom you work for. And I happen to work for a fantastic senior fellow who cultivates my interests in areas like domestic terrorism and national security by allowing me to work on his projects. A typical day might consist of writing for my boss's blog and editing posts, or conducting research for the books that he's working on. I could also be busy with administrative tasks like scheduling and phone calls. And if any kind of work that requires a written draft comes up, I'm usually the first one to take a crack at it.

What do you consider to be the most enlivening aspect of your job?

I feel like I'm learning a lot about the kind of career that I want to have, what it's like to have a career in the policy world in Washington DC. Both Brookings and the city are incredibly stimulating to be around. And at the end of the day, the reality is that I'm working on issues that I care deeply about.

Now, long before you set up shop in DC, you were living and attending primary school in Bangkok.

Well, as a kid, the school that I went to for the first 12 years of my education was an American International School. So I grew up thinking that going to college was a possibility for me. Though I didn't start thinking about it seriously until tenth grade. That's when I decided that I sincerely wanted to pursue higher education in the states. I realized that I'd have so many more career options if I came to the U.S. I spent my junior year of high school researching and applying to different schools. Some of them were in Asia, but I absolutely wanted to come to U.S.

Did you already have a firm grasp of what you wanted to study?

Actually, my interests were pretty similar to what I'm doing now. I was fascinated with global politics and international affairs, that type of stuff. I can still remember this one day in high school when I thought, "Hmm, I'd like to work for the UN."

Tell me about the college application process. It's such a nightmare domestically that I'm kind of embarrassed to imagine what it must be like for international students.

It was *completely* different than the way you'd apply to college in the states. As an international applicant, there are no college visits or open houses, so the entire process is essentially taking a shot in the dark. A lot of my decisions boiled down to college rankings and websites. I tried to pick schools that seemed to suit my academic interests and offer an interesting campus life. There were also some admissions counselors that would visit the Bangkok area, and a Skidmore representative happened to visit my school. I got a sense of what school I might prefer through meeting these people. But it was still a guessing game. I mean, I could have been very unhappy at Skidmore but thankfully, it worked out well.

Once you set foot on the Skidmore campus, after months of interviews and applications, how did you feel at first?

It was so long ago...I'm trying to remember. I was so happy to be there. Freshman year was pretty overwhelming but then again, everyone's freshman year is. But in terms of being in a new country, people often ask me if it was really hard and my answer is no, not really. Because I was so excited and there was so much going on around campus that I would usually be too distracted to step back and think, "Whoa, this is tough."

How long did it take you to feel acclimatized to America?

Getting cultured was pretty easy for me. I'm sure there were moments where I felt self-conscious early on, because I didn't know much about the States. I hadn't seen much of the landscape. Not only was I a newbie to the country, but I was also living in a small town, attending a small school. So, life was a little hard at first. I don't think I talked a lot about my background or upbringing during those early months. I just focused on assimilating myself into the States.

As your friendships and social network developed, did you eventually feel more inclined to share your past experiences growing up abroad?

Yeah, as I became more comfortable with my best friends and myself, I also became more comfortable talking about my upbringing. It's hard to talk about it because people who've grown up in the U.S. can't relate that much. But my friends could relate to *me* and my personal qualities, which was the key to opening up that other part of myself.

How did the academic road eventually lead you to the Brookings Institute?

When I came to Skidmore, I fell in love with the government department. After declaring my major and working with mentors, I spent my sophomore summer working in Washington DC, which exposed me to life there. I fell in love with this city. It was the best summer of my life, and I knew that I wanted to go back. So, the next summer, I applied and was hired for an internship with the Brookings Institute. And it was a great experience. I was working in terrorism and national security research. The position gave me professional exposure to a lot of new fields, and ultimately, I think it got me through the door further down the road. By the spring of senior year, I was applying for *lot* of different jobs, throwing everything against the wall and seeing what stuck. As an international student, you can't be in a state for more than 60 days after you're done with college.

You only get 60 days to find a job? In this economy?

If you're an international student doing undergrad or a master's degree, you're on an F1 visa, which allows you to stay in US for the years you're studying and it also gives you one year extra, which is called "optional practical training" or "OPT" for short. So for me, it was four years to study, and one year to work. But you actually have to apply for OPT, which is a bit stupid since it theoretically comes with your visa. You apply for it close to graduation. So that was an added stress, especially because you can't start work until you have an OPT! Ultimately, it comes down to a lot of paperwork, and if you switch jobs for any reason, you have to inform the government. So there's not much flexibility.

What kind of restrictions does an OPT carry?

Your job has to be connected to the subject you were studying. So I had to find a job with a strong international affairs or governmental focus. I couldn't go work in business, ring up customers at a McDonald's, or even babysit, since none of those were within my field of study. Either you get a job or you leave the country in 60 days. You could still do volunteer work or intern after 60 days, but that wasn't an option for me. I needed the money and had to find a source of income. I didn't have the option of going home and crashing with my parents while I got my feet on the ground. And right before graduation, something opened up at Brookings for three months: a paid internship. It was a godsend.

But how did you feel about the end date attached to the position?

At first I was a little stressed by the three month time period, knowing I'd soon have to find something else, but I didn't have any other jobs lined up, and of course, the economy was shit. So I decided to go for it. I was especially lucky that they offered me the job, since a lot of organizations won't even consider international students if they know you only have a year of OPT. I mean...why would they hire someone with such a short window of availability? Most entry-level jobs last around 2-3 years. I didn't really feel settled at Brookings until after four months.

And yet, they kept you on after the internship ended.

They did! Brookings wanted to keep me on for longer, but what most nonprofits can or can't do depends on money. So I was really nervous. But after the first month and a half of my job, funding came through that would allow my job to turn into a yearlong position. And I was thrilled. I really wanted to stay in the States, at Brookings, and I loved the people I was working with and what we were doing. Now, I'd be a research assistant until June of 2012.

But again, you had another employment deadline on the horizon, albeit further away than the last one. Let's fast-forward one year...

As June 20th, 2012 was nearing, I sat down with my boss and we talked about what our options were. I couldn't stay at Brookings or in the U.S. anymore on my F1 Visa. It was finished. So my only option was to get an H-1B Visa.[1] Lots of people have them but it was something that would depend largely on my boss because it costs every company a lot of money.

How much?

A couple thousand dollars to sponsor an international worker. That's a significant amount of money and there are also liability issues: the employer is basically responsible for the visa carrier professionally. It's also difficult because your employer has to show the government that

---

[1] The H-1B is a non-immigrant visa that allows a foreign worker with specialized skills to work for a U.S. employer for a set period of time.

you have a unique set of skills that the organization requires. Because the government wants to make sure companies aren't just hiring international workers when they could be hiring US citizens to do the same jobs.

So how did your supervisors make this happen?

My boss spoke to the vice president of Brookings, who then met with our legal counsel. They had to make a determination about whether I was valuable enough to sponsor. And in the end, they decided they wanted to do that, which I feel very fortunate about. My H-1B lets me stay here for two years and it started last June. And you can renew it three times, so hypothetically, I could work here for up to six years.

Now that you've been working in the U.S. for a few years, how welcoming do you feel America is or isn't to international students and workers?

I've felt very welcomed and accepted by the majority of people I've met here. Although, I did spend the last five in New York and DC, both of which are progressive places with lots of workers and students from overseas. If there's any disconnect, it's that most people don't understand how challenging it is to fight to stay in the US. That issue feels very much like my battle. Immigration reform is near and dear to the hearts of many coworkers at Brookings, not to mention, my own. Historically, I think the U.S. has done a fine job of making it easy for people to come here, but for the last 20-25 years, that hasn't been the case at all.

Looking ahead, in the next five or ten years, what do you hope to be doing with your life?

I'd like to build a career in the States doing national security policy work focused on Southeast Asia. I'm not an American citizen, which limits the places I could go to pursue future endeavors, including any domestic or international policy work.

Drawing from your professional experiences here—and those of your peers—how do you identify with the term "Millennial?"

Based on the people I've been around, I think it means being very flexible and open to a lot of different things, whether it's moving across the country or jumping into a completely new line of work. Most people I know, they don't have one major or passion anymore. They don't graduate into a job that they hold for the next 30 years. They learn to be very resilient. Today's economy seems to favor people who can be resilient and adapt to expectations and environmental factors that are constantly changing.

JEFF

25 years old
Farmhand
Lafayette, Colorado

July 4, 2013

EXTERIOR. A vast field of broccoli crops. Workers hack at the stems with sharp knives. The sun is merciless. The surrounding landscape is bone dry.

What brought you to Lafayette and, more specifically, to this broccoli field we're standing in?

My whole family's been involved in farming for as long as I can remember. Growing up in Central Pennsylvania, I got to know my way around feed bins, harvesters, the like. And you know, when you're a kid and you want to break out from the mold your parents set before you...that's originally what I saw myself doing. Breaking away from farming. I studied information technology in college, two-year program, and did the whole young person in the city thing in Pittsburgh for almost a year. But the quality of life wasn't worth it. I was broke too much, contract work was hard to get, I made ends meet by working at a sports bar a lot of the time. I started looking for an escape plan and that's when I started hearing about life in Colorado from friends who'd gone out there to ski-bum for the winter and never left. Well, some of them did, but not the majority.

And what did these enrapturing stories involve that appealed to you so much?

Oh man, just, like...working outdoors all day, going hiking, drinking and brewing great beer, seeing concerts and art shows any given week. I'd like to say it was something more noble that interested me, like getting back with nature, but at the time, I was really just looking to inject some R&R into my life. You know? Anything but this cold, competitive city thing. It wasn't a life plan or anything, but I was only 24, so fuck it, right? And my student loans were manageable since I went to a community college, so if I could just find a job that paid even slightly above minimum wage, getting out west would be feasible.

And that's how you found yourself working as full-time farmhand?

Right. It was kind of a full circle thing, but the first job lead I came across was through a friend of a Facebook friend who'd already worked for a year on the farm. If you'd asked me before I moved to Pittsburgh, if I could've pictured myself putting on gloves and Carhartts again, heading into the fields at sunrise, I would've laughed. But the more this person and I talked about the farm job, the more real it felt: the possibility of taking it and starting a new life. Plus, after being in the city for a while...there was an aspect of working on a farm that meshed well with thoughts and feelings I'd had lately.

What sort of feelings?

Well, I guess...I guess you could say it was this feeling that living in modern society—especially in city areas—demands that we all buy into this big system of exploitation. Of people, land, and other natural resources. And so, my being open to getting back into farming, in Lafayette and the greater Boulder area...it was wanting to take myself out of that system. Helping to provide a way for people to get food that was healthier and more social.

So how was it, reintegrating yourself into this intensely physical lifestyle after college and a few years of bartending?

It sucked. [laughs] I mean, it sucked at first. Even as a kid, growing up, I'd never worked full-time on a farm. I knew what kind of sleep schedule to expect, but it's impossible to understand the agony of pulling up weeds for hours under the sun until you've spent the better part of a week doing that. First time I sliced my finger with a harvesting knife, hacking broccoli crops...that was a rite of passage. I've still got a scar. Didn't need stitches, but still...

Does the Boulder area provide a quality of life that's superior to what you left?

Oh, definitely. I mean, I work a bare minimum 40 hours a week here, and I mean *work*. But, the cost of living is so much better. Even within Boulder. That's where I'm based right now. A bunch of us are. We carpool out to the farm in the early morning. But when we're not working, we're still outside most of the time. Running the Flatirons has become my conquest. I didn't even run much before getting out here, but in Boulder, if you haven't worked out at least twice a day, you're basically lazy. It's insane.

How long do you think you'd like to stay here?

Probably not the rest of my life. My roots are still in Pennsylvania and when I feel ready to maybe start my own farming operation...that's really something I can imagine myself doing now...it would be easier for me to get started back there. I mean, sure, there's the Amish issue.

The Amish issue?

Well, if you're a farmer in Pennsylvania, your competition is the Amish. Since they don't live in a modern way, they don't have modern equipment to maintain, or modern lifestyles to pay for. That lets them charge lower prices. Prices we couldn't charge if we wanted to turn a profit and be paid fairly.

I was going to ask about pay. Are you compensated sufficiently as a farm laborer?

It's a good deal. I'm not making bank here, but I like the job, I can pay my bills, and I've got health insurance because of the state subsidies. I mean, that *should* be the bottom line for all farmhands, but we both know it's not. Especially with the places that employ undocumented workers and pay them shit. Again, it's exploitation, and it's pretty common. Colorado's gotten tougher with fighting that, but even around here, you hear stories and see things.

Thinking about your agricultural ambition, what type of farming are you interested in?

Livestock. I think we're on the verge of a big comeback for meat. Out here, the market for organic meat is big. Way bigger than anything back east. And in general, the old stigma against meat eaters seems to be fading away. I also learned a bit about the livestock trade by helping out with my relatives' farming operations, when I was growing up. Stuff like mob grazing. That's this technique where you take cattle, and instead of keeping them in one penned range, you move the whole herd to different plots of land each day. The idea is, you're imitating the old days when bison roamed from place to place, eating grass with different nutrients and passing it out again, back onto the land. It's healthier for the cows.

So, you've already got a heft of secondhand knowledge when it comes to the types of farming you're interested in. I'd imagine that's what would make it easier to get started with your own operation back in Pennsylvania. Being closer to that knowledge well.

Some, yeah. My family's still active in livestock farming, so it wouldn't be a stretch to move back eventually and work some more before going out on my own. That's my hope. But all trends and know-how aside, the next 10 or 15 years are gonna be pretty complicated, when it comes to meat production and growing food in general. At least, out here it'll be complicated.

How so?

Water. [pause] That's what keeps me up at night. Water. It's pretty hot out here, right?

Yeah. I don't know how you get used to this. I'm from New England. Since we started talking, I've had to wring sweat from my shirt. Twice.

Everyone talks about California as the drought zone, but it's happening around here too, man. Hotter summers, less rain...I don't think the snowmelt issue has hit us in the same way, but still, it takes gallons and gallons of water just to raise one cow. And water around here is getting more expensive for farms to use. Plus, we're also giving away a lot of our state water to California. They siphon it right off the Colorado River, so...[laughs] That's not gonna end well.

Has there been pushback against the state government over sharing resources like that? It might be the right thing to do, but the optics isn't great. Especially if your generalized take on California is "that place where the Kardashians and tech bros frolic."

For sure. People aren't happy about it, but I

mean...that's part of the contract of being a coalition of states, right? Helping each other out with resources, in hard times.

So then, you do have faith in the government being able to mitigate hardship when times get drastic and tough.

Uh...yes and no. My grandparents were very big into unions. They were alive during the FDR years. Even my own folks, they were more pro-government than a lot of our neighbors. So, there's the faith that I grew up with. But ever since coming out here, and seeing how much Colorado supports local farmers compared to other states...not just the state government, but the people too...I guess you could say my faith in government has become more localized. This is a good state to start a farm in, and that's mainly because of the reasonable property taxes, the available land, and how willing people are to pay for organic food. Local government's definitely a part of that equation. But bigger government, on a federal level...

They're not as in tune?

It's not even being in or out of tune. It feels like the federal government doesn't even care about trying to work for the majority of the people. One thing I often forget is...we're a fucking enormous country. Finding solutions that are gonna please everyone, when people have such different views on everything from the environment to healthcare to taxes...it's a tough job, for sure. And sometimes it feels like our leaders have just given up. You know? It's like, these days, if left to their own devices, they can't be trusted to do *anything* in the public interest. Most of the laws passed in the last few years seem designed to please corporations and billionaires. So, in that sense, no, I don't trust the federal government to look out for regular people. I'm starting to think that giving more power to state governments might be our best hope.

I've thought about that too. But what would happen if a state does something objectively unjust like bring back some equivalent of Jim Crow? Or, if one state revamped its energy laws to be more environmentally friendly, and a neighboring state did the opposite and the resulting pollution trickled across state lines...

That's what sucks. It's not a perfect solution, by any means. We all have to share this country, but it's like people are becoming more and more unwilling to do that, even when our model of government depends on it.

[The two of us notice squealing from a nearby creek. We tread over to find a group of teenagers floating down the river in big inner tubes.]

That's funny. You don't usually get tubers out here. Most of them shoot down Boulder Creek. You start up in the canyon and go from there.

Is it dangerous?

I mean, there's some rocks you gotta watch out for. Couple of big ones right under the surface of the water at the start. But it's fine. You just gotta be sure you're not on the river when the 100-year flood goes down. [laughs]

Is the 100-year flood exactly what it sounds like?

Oh yeah. [nods towards the mountains] So, like, every century or so, there's a big washout of melted snow and rainwater from up in the mountains. Comes down through the valley and goes right through Boulder. Last time it happened, forests got wiped out. Whole fucking city was submerged for days. That was back in...I think it was the late 1800s. So, technically, we're overdue. [laughs]

Does that worry you? Knowing that you could lose your home?

Sometimes. End of the world could happen any day now. It's a long time coming, I guess.

STEPHANIE

26 years old
Student
Denton, Texas

July 11, 2013

INTERIOR. A shrimp joint. Sawdust-on-the-floor kind of place. Metallic clanging and shouting reverberate from the kitchen. The dining room is festooned with holiday lights. Students pack it.

The first thing that struck me when we emailed each other was your change of study. You went from biology to...philosophy? Why? How?

I spent the majority of my undergrad years at Eckerd College just living and breathing science. And I wound up spending a lot of time with my professors. To a certain degree, I liked talking to them more than I liked talking to my peers. Hearing about their real life experiences as working scientists was an interesting contrast to the more knowledge-based science that we discussed in class. During my senior year of college, I was accepted into an apprentice program for aspiring educators. I was required to select an academic advisor for my final school year, and...I chose a philosophy professor.

Just for the hell of it? Or was there a deliberate motive?

I thought it would be really interesting to work with a mentor outside my major. And at first, I don't think Eckerd knew what do with me. This was the first time I'd really encountered the term "interdisciplinary. And it was also what took me to Denton, to UNT.[1] My advising professor at Eckerd,

---

[1] "UNT" is how the University of North Texas is referred to by almost everyone in Denton.

Dr. Bruce Foltz, introduced me to a colleague at UNT's philosophy department who happened to be seeking driven research assistants. When Bruce told me about the job, his explanation was that this friend of his was having a hard time finding good help for the coming semester. It was almost a year later when I found out that this wasn't true at all: that Bruce had flat-out recommended me. They offered me the job! So I called him up like, "You! You dirty dog." He's an amazing man.

How did you feel about the prospect of moving halfway across the country and devoting yourself to an entirely new field of study?

My parents were definitely concerned. And I couldn't blame them. For years, I had this plan to move on from Eckerd and become a career scientist with good prospects for the future. And the position at UNT was only part-time, so...my parents were worried about the financial stress it might entail. But I worked out a temporary living arrangement with my aunt, who's based in Dallas, and that made the transition easier. I started commuting to school and by the time the apprentice program was over, I'd begun my master's studies at UNT and found a place to live up here.

And once you began getting into your philosophy studies...what was that like? How did it feel to be in such a different sort of intellectual space?

The first three months here were extremely intense, but so rewarding. I had never been around so many professors who were audibly thinking about the ethos of science at all waking hours. It was a really refreshing tonic from the more clinical fact-based approach I'd taken in my undergraduate years and even back in high school. All my presuppositions about the relationship between scientists, the public, and lawmakers...they were just deconstructed.

What was your most stubborn presupposition, going into UNT?

I think it's *still* the kind of attitude with which scientists approach uncertainty and risk. Whether something is an obstacle or an opportunity. In many ways, I had been trained to fear the subjective for most of my scientific upbringing. And yet, the subjective aspects, when it comes to policymaking, are extremely important. What I'm learning now is that hard scientific facts alone are usually not enough to facilitate smart policy decisions. The final outcome is almost always based on social values or special interests.

As far as political issues go—issues that are vulnerable to social values and special interests—what's something that you find yourself discussing with students and colleagues?

The issue of greenwashing is something that comes up quite often around here. It's very trendy and palatable for a company to say their products are organic, natural, eco-friendly, etc. But often, if you dig deeper, you'll find that this whole "going green" makeover is just a packaging strategy. Like whitewashing, it's just painting over something to obscure what's really underneath, which is usually pollution and exploitation. And the only reason this is happening is because more people are making shopping decisions based on changing values about what it means to be a "good" consumer. That's how the philosophical angle comes into focus. How do we live ethically in a time of increasing pollution and privatization?

Someone I met recently mentioned something I think you'd be heartened to hear. I asked them what their greatest fear for the future was, and they just said, "Water."

Good! It's hard to imagine people remaining apathetic to environmental destruction when something vital as water is endangered.

Right, but it's already endangered. And people are still denying that anything is wrong with our ecosystem. [pause] This is probably simplistic thinking, but I wonder what would happen if we had more young, well-informed people in public office who could really appreciate the urgency of the situation. Do you see yourself going down that road? Into policy?

I've thought about it. Our society likes to build up science as this career path toward changing the world. But one of the realities I'm finding is that academic research rarely ever makes it beyond academic institutions. So I thought approaching science from a philosophical place could be a way of training myself to think and communicate well. To insert myself into political circles one day. Maybe that could make a difference, but...[pause]...there's something about policy work that gives me pause. Policy is meant to address norms and expectations. And I'm not sure if I have the kind of hubris it takes to define what can be the norm for 350 million Americans with *extremely* diverse opinions and ideas of what the world is.

And yet, there's still this impulse people have, to homogenize define human experience in black and white terms. Look at all the ongoing cultural debate about human nature. Are we hardwired to be sociopathic or compassionate? I don't think the answer's so simple.

And that's the trouble! As a policymaker, you *have* to simplify all those complexities of life into one shared idea. One common interest.

So what's the solution?

Well, I think a neat idea would be imagining what the common interest *could* be 500 years from now, and letting that inform your present-day policy recommendations.

So then, what do you think the common interest in 500 years might look be?

Hmm. [pause] Maybe recognizing and respecting differences? Taking diversity of thought and experience seriously, as a good thing.

I wish we could have the Bloomberg editorial board listening in on this conversation. Just to offer them another take on what Millennials are thinking and talking about. I don't think either of us has brought up smartphones or Facebook since we started talking.

Give it time. We're not done yet.

Right. It could all go downhill from here. But seriously, when you read the adjectives that are often attached to people our age - entitled, lazy, apathetic - how do you relate to those popular characterizations? What do they suggest about Millennials?

Actually, I think those characterizations are a lot more telling of Boomers than Millennials. It feels like this projection of fears the Boomers must have, over what the future will look like for their kids. As if they were saying, "We've worked very hard to make this world for you and now you're telling us that *you don't want it?!*"

But, one could argue that the Boomers didn't preserve the opportunity and prosperity they inherited. The U.S. has outsourced millions of jobs, our environment appears to be in disarray due to emissions, and there's talk of privatizing social security.

Sure. There's a kind of selfishness at work, sure. You could say a lot of Boomers only thought of the short term. To set up a house in the suburbs, a car, and all these technological gadgets as evidence of a good life...it's just not sustainable! So when some Boomers talk about providing a "better" life for their kids, I see it as this intensification of all the conveniences they grew up with. Which, we're realizing now, aren't indicative of a good life at all.

Give me an example of one of those conveniences.

How about coffee? Right here in Denton, we get coffee from all over the world. It's grown by people we'll never meet and we don't know anything about their working conditions: whether they *want* to be laborers. We invest a lot of trust that the processes by which coffee is made and transported to us are sustainable. That they'll always bring us rich, delicious coffee whenever we want. But that trust can be broken, and for something that's not a *necessity*...[pause] It really worries me at times.

Why do you think this introspective side of our generation...the thoughtful, concerned, cognizant of the future side...why do you think that's rarely acknowledged in the media and conversations that essentially pathologize Millennials as entitled and narcissistic dipshits?

Maybe it's a way of deflecting the responsibility some Boomers feel, for the world they're handing over to Millennials. I would imagine there's a really strong resistance against accepting any blame for the way the world looks now. [chuckles] You know, this is something that Plato was talking about in ancient Athens. We express regret over the ways we live when we become most intimately concerned with death. In the opening of The Republic, the old patriarch of the household is only around briefly because he has to go attend human sacrifices. He represents the old guard: religious authority, that's now starting to wane in Athens. The younger members of the conversation are more interested in exercising individual freedom.

I like where you're going with this.

So, Socrates goes up to the older gentleman and he says, "You're in a condition all of us will face in our lives: you're old. What's it like to be old."

And what does the patriarch say?

He says, "I sometimes think that everything will be okay. That there's nothing to worry about because I have enough money to settle all the wrongs I've committed over the years, and enter the afterlife with a clear conscience. But if there's no afterlife...when I think about that possibility, I'm stuck with this terrible fear that wakes me in the middle of the night, disrupts my activities, and fills me with a sense of deep despair. And I question why I've lived my life that way I have."

BEN

25 years old
Police Officer
Troy, Ohio

July 25, 2013

INTERIOR. A Dodge Charger, parked beside a field. The afternoon is muggy and the air is full of tiny winged ants. Thunderclouds are gathering.

When did you first become fixated with law enforcement, as a career?

The original plan was always for me to attend college first. Education was a priority in my family. We were pretty solid middle class. So that's what I did, and I majored in criminal justice. My parents were able to offer some support, but I also paid my own way through, working part-time. And as I began taking classes, I took up an interest in government. So, I figured, there was the possibility of attending law school and going into politics. But I didn't like the idea of being holed up in an office, cut off from the real world.

Specifically, what was it about that occupational lifestyle, about being "cut off" that rubbed you the wrong way?

I like dealing with people. I'm a really social person, I think it's fun to interact, and I didn't want a job where I'd be sitting behind a computer for most of the day, chatting with people at the water cooler, if I was lucky. I wanted to be out there...I know this sounds corny, but I wanted to be helping people. You get a lot of that in police work.

So, after you finished college...walk me along the path that took you to your first job as a police officer.

I enrolled in a police academy where we covered all aspects of training. It's not easy. Lots of exams. They pepper spray you and shoot you with a Taser. Both of those things are required as a part of the certification procedure. They do it so you'll understand how the other guy's gonna feel, and hopefully you use both weapons carefully. And all the while, learning all this, I was working private security gigs to pay the bills. When I finished, I applied for a deputy job with the City of Troy Police Department, and I got it.

How did it feel to take lessons you absorbed in an academic environment and apply them to the real world?

It was kind of terrifying. You go from this environment where you've got some control over where you're going, and then suddenly, you're on your own. During the first day on the job, my field training officer drove me out to a rural area and asked me, point-blank, "Do you want to do this job?"

And what did you tell him?

I said, "I don't know," and my FTO officer said, "That's the best answer you could have given." And that was an interesting lesson. 90% of the time you're in the field, you're going to have to consult with somebody else. It's alright to be unsure. I mean...the whole process of being assigned to a call is pretty nerve-wracking. You see each call pop up on the computer screen in your squad car. And if you're thinking, "Jeez, I'm not sure what to do in this situation," you start praying that *your* number won't get picked to address the call. But when it happens, you hit the ground running and learn from the hands-on experience.

Can you remember the first call you responded to?

Yeah. It was a civil protection order violation. This guy was calling up his ex-girlfriend, in violation of a court order that forbade him from doing that. Pretty simple. The guy didn't want to be cooperative on the phone, so we had go out and talk to him. And of course, that was something I didn't look forward to.

Were you alone?

My FTO officer went out with me on that call. And before we got out of the car to go knock on the guy's door, he told me something else that's really important. Most of the people you're going to be dealing with are repeat offenders. They've indulged in criminal activity for a long time. But they only represent about 1% of the population. The thing you've got to realize is that this job can make you extremely cynical of people, the way they act. And since this country is for the people, by the people...that's something to be avoided at all costs.

So, how do you avoid feeling like that? How do you keep all the ugliness you encounter from darkening your outlook on people?

I've got a half hour drive home each day. So I just crank up the music, roll down the windows, whatever. Little things like that can help you drain the adrenaline. Because some of the calls we get…things like babies choking, you're racing there and you have no idea whether you'll be dealing with a living, breathing kid by the time you show up. And if everything's okay, you're thrilled. But the stress still leaves a mental mark on you. It's just…like…having good friends and loved ones, people you can talk to, that really helps too. And on my days off, I'll go swimming, catch a movie, play golf, go running.

When your job gets difficult, what keeps you committed, other than civic obligation?

What I really like about my job is that it can be rewarding in ways that you don't imagine. You show up on a scene where someone's distraught because some mom's boyfriend is getting in a big fight and she's torn between him and her kids. To most people, that shouldn't be a big question, but you come in, you defuse the situation, try to take the grief away from both parties. And to me, that's really rewarding: to have people actually thank you for your time and effort. There's a lot of work out there where you rarely get that kind of thanks.

Do you feel that the community here is generally appreciative of your efforts?

Actually, if I'm being straight, we don't get thanked *that* often. The running joke here is, "If you want the thanks, go be a firefighter." Because sometimes we have to do things that don't sit well with people. Like taking some well-liked guy to jail.

That's something I've wondered about. With respect to our generation, how you think most Millennials perceive police officers and other law enforcement professionals?

Good question. I'd say we're not perceived very well. I mean, even when I was growing up, I'd watch movies that would always feature the jerk cop who ruins everyone's fun. And the memory of that has definitely influenced the way I carry myself in the field.

How so?

Moderation is important. In some situations, force and assertive actions are necessary. But let's say I'm pulling someone over for speeding. If they're doing 50 miles over the speed limit, they're gonna hear about it. But if they're only 10 miles over, I'll probably give them a warning. It's all about putting yourself in the other person's shoes and trying to remember where they're coming from. At the end of the day, we're here to serve and protect, not to rule.

I'm sure you're well aware of this, but a lot of people are concerned with these recent accounts of officers acting aggressively, not exercising moderation, and not aiming for this sort of mutual respect between cop and constituent that you're talking about. Shooting first, asking questions later. Do you ever worry about this?

Well, you can't really blame the media for focusing on these stories. They're corporations and they're gonna go for any news that attracts the most eyeballs and riles people up. It's all about perception. A lot of us here in Troy, we choose to wear our bulletproof vests underneath our dress shirts. Because if you're walking around with all this protective gear and these ammo magazines attached to your exterior, it does look more militaristic. It changes your relationship with the community.

Indeed. I'd feel occupied if my local police force walked around dressed like that.

One thing I've talked to a lot of my constituents about is our response time. In a city, you can respond to a fellow officer in seconds, but out here, it can take upwards of 10 or 15 minutes. Not knowing how long it'll take to for backup to arrive can be scary for an officer on duty. It can be the deciding factor between approaching a suspect calmly or drawing your gun and shouting "Get out of the car now! Don't look at me! Keep your hands above your head!" So, in our department, we try to discourage that line of thinking. Like I said earlier, this system is by the people, for the people. And if we approach everyone as a violent suspect, then the whole thing it won't work anymore.

"People say, 'If you don't vote then you have no right to complain.' Well where's the logic in that?"

George Carlin
George Carlin: Jammin' In New York, 1992

KATIE & LANDON

22 and 23 years old
Unemployed
Las Vegas, Nevada

July 1, 2013

INTERIOR. A Greyhound bus. Midafternoon. The red southwestern landscape sails by outside. The bus is half full. Most of the passengers are asleep.

Where are you both going today?

LANDON: Salt Lake City. I'd like to say it's just a visit, but...we're picking up and trying something new.

KATIE: Vegas is home for both of us. *Was* home, I mean. We went to the same high school back then. Got together at prom and that was it. We were thinking of getting married last year, actually, but-

LANDON: Wasn't a good situation.

Were you too busy with work? Or was it something else?

KATIE: I wish work had been the problem.

LANDON: Well, it pretty much *was* the fucking problem.

KATIE: His family's business went under. It was really bad.

What sort of business did your family own, Landon?

LANDON: My folks had a chain of vacuum cleaner stores. There were six locations in the Vegas area. Seems pretty unreal to think about that right now, but...for a time...it made us a good living. I had a comfortable childhood. I was the manager of one of them. Did that since I was 17, up until about six months ago. You know how much I made last year? Before taxes?

How much?

LANDON: $46,000. I mean, for a retail job, that's pretty good, right?

KATIE: We had an apartment together on the north side. Two bedroom. It was a deal when we got it, but with Landon's salary and mine together-

What were you doing for work at the time, Katie?

KATIE: Also retail. I'd bounced around a couple places. Most recently, this fancy cookware place that also gave cooking lessons. I was looking into doing that up until recently. I've always been good at cooking. I like meeting new people.

Evidently. Otherwise, I'd probably be stuck next to the guy with McNugget breath who took the seat beside mine.

KATIE: That's the last, worst resort. Fast food. Never in a thousand years. I, uh, I had a friend who worked at a Burger King during school. Every time they came to class, it was, like...you could smell the fat on them. He probably showered twice a day and you could still smell it.

LANDON: Better than riding this toilet.

KATIE: What's that, babe?

LANDON: You don't smell that? Take a whiff.

[The three of us take a moment sniff the air. Indeed, a strong fecal odor has begun to spread throughout the bus. At the rear of the coach, the bathroom door swings open ominously. We've got a long to go until Salt Lake City.]

So...there's no easy way to ask: why are you two moving to Salt Lake City? Did the family business going out change things irreparably? What sunk the business?

LANDON: Bad economy. Six months after the real estate market goes down, we have to shutter two of our stores. My folks had a lot of their savings riding on real estate. But that's not all. People are feeling the squeeze far and wide, so...just...business goes down. Revenue goes down. We have to lay people off just to keep the doors open, but everything's short-staffed. And at the end of the day...

KATIE: People aren't spending. Not like they used to.

LANDON: By 2011, we've closed five locations. All we've got left is the flagship. So my folks sit down, they do a big old cost-benefit analysis, and guess what? It's cheaper to sell the store than it is to keep it running.

Did your folks get a fair offer from someone?

LANDON: I don't really know what's fair for a business like that, but whatever the offer was...most of the money's gone now. Credit cards. Mortgage payments. My folks had a lot of debt. Like, way more than either of us realized. And that's when the worst of them really came out.

KATIE: There was this one dinner, and they started fighting about something stupid...like, getting someone to fix the dryer. It had been stopping and starting. And from there...it just turned into this big blowup. It was ugly. I mean, really ugly.

LANDON: That was a fucked up night. I never saw my parents actually *hit* each other before. It was like, after the stores were gone...it was almost like they started becoming different people, and right there, they just exploded.

What do you think it was that changed their dynamic so drastically?

LANDON: I think they were just spazzing out. Taking the financial stuff out on each other. I mean, I didn't know what to do. At some point, all you've got left is just sitting back and waiting for the end to come.

So they separated?

LANDON: Divorced. My mom's in Reno with her sisters. Dad's still in Vegas.

KATIE: But there's nothing for us back in Vegas. He's out of work, his family's fucked, and we can't live on my income. They cut my hours to part-time so they didn't have to pay for my health insurance. And there's barely any other jobs for him to take either.

Even with the tourism economy that Vegas is famous for?

KATIE: Nothing. For every busboy opening, there's, like, 30 people in line. You can't even get work at any of the shithole casinos where people go to shoot up in the restrooms and take poppers.

So then, you guys will find jobs once you get to Salt Lake?

LANDON: Something. Anything's gotta be better than Vegas right now."

KATIE: My mom lives there now. She's gonna help us get on our feet for the first month, but from there, we're on our own.

Why do you think the job market's so bad in Vegas? Or most places? I mean, you two probably hear it as much as I do, some politician goes on the air and harps about

*how "the economy is recovering." But I don't know too
many folks who've felt that recovery yet.*

KATIE: It's such bullshit. What are they talking
about? Who's this "recovery" supposed to be for?
Not people like us.

LANDON: I'd say it's mostly Obama's fault. The
media's not telling it like it is, but the guy's moving
our country towards socialism. That's a big
problem. It's no wonder you've got businesses
closing their doors.

KATIE: At this point, I just don't even listen when
Obama or any politician talks about fixing
everything. They're not serious. They don't have
skin in the game.

*You mean they're not really invested in finding solutions
because they're not feeling the pain that the two of you
have experienced? That anyone who's lost their job, their
home, or their savings is grappling with?*

KATIE: Yeah. And then they ask you to vote for
them and give them money so they can run a
campaign, and you're like..."Fuck you. You don't
care. This isn't important to you. My life isn't
important to you."

LANDON: I don't have a problem with some of
the things Obama's done. Gay marriage, that sort
of thing...fine by me. But when it comes to
business...I just don't see how making it more

expensive to operate a business is gonna make it easier for people to keep their heads above water. The whole thing with her hours getting slashed, that's all because of the healthcare law. Just another cost to shoulder if you run a business.

Running a business: is that something you've thought about doing in the future?

LANDON: Yeah, definitely. It was something I thought about when I was working last. I didn't really have that perfect idea yet, but managing my own staff, finances...yeah, it's interesting to me. But now, I'll be lucky if I can find *a* job when we get to SLC.

When you two arrive in Salt Lake and get relatively settled...what would an optimal future look like? What do you hope to achieve and enjoy there?

LANDON: A place to live, just the two of us. That's a start. Jobs that don't turn us into assholes. I'm open to staying long term if things work out.

KATIE: I just want to feel like...like we're not running a race against...I don't know the right words to describe what we're running against. But it's not good, whatever the thing is.

MARTIN

25 years old
Office Assistant
New Orleans, Louisiana

May 25, 2015

EXTERIOR. A city park. The last hour's worth of sunlight flares through the trees. Insects buzz in the branches above. The humidity saturates all.

You were in New Orleans right around the time that Hurricane Katrina made landfall.

I wasn't here during the actual storm. I left a few days earlier, but I did live here at the time, so...I suffered all of the losses. If you know a New Orleans native, or really just people that deal with hurricanes in general, we don't really leave for most storms because it's just wind and rain. A lot of people don't pack up because they figure it's not worth the gas or the time. They hunker down in their homes and a few days without power go by and then it's all over. But before Katrina...it was crazy because nobody knew the exact path that the storm was supposed to take or even how big it was. And it covered the entire Gulf of Mexico and got stronger because of the warm water and climate throughout the Gulf.

When the enormity of the storm became clear, what happened? How did people react?

The whole city pretty much went crazy, like, two days before the storm. My family and I decided to get out, so we headed to Georgia, which...probably wasn't the best decision. Because you're driving *into* the storm, parallel to the coast where it made landfall. [laughs] So in that way, we did get to experience Katrina, while driving to Savannah.

But...yeah. It was scary. I had a lot of friends who got displaced from their families. They were just placed on buses and sent away to different locations. I have friends who were living in the Superdome after the storm, texting me all kinds of stuff. I had a neighbor, across the street from my house, who texted my mom during the storm to say that she could see...that my stepdad had left his briefcase on my mom's couch. Because the couch was floating down the street, with the briefcase on top of it. And the neighbor was on her rooftop, watching all of this happen.

Were you able to avoid catastrophic damage?

Well, the water settled at 12 feet, which basically...we had a one-story house, so the water settled into the ceilings, and the roof. So, we came back to nothing. All the stuff you hold dear, toys, clothes, electronics, your room. It was really hard. And that was just me. The fact that a lot of my friends are still here is, like, a miracle.

How long did it take for you and your family to rebuild your lives?

I don't know if we'll ever get back to how we used to be. I mean...I was 13 when Katrina happened, and I didn't even want to come back when I saw what happened to our house. So we ended up coming back and resettling in an area called St. Rose, Louisiana. And it took about a good year and a half before our lives just, kind of got back to normal. I remember helping my parents doing construction work on the house we moved into, which was a lot of work. But socially...it's still not like it used be. My old neighborhood, you go over there and it still looks like Katrina happened yesterday. A lot of the people we knew, they still haven't come back. I don't know if they ever will. And it's kind of frustrating how a lot of the people moving here now act like they know so much about the city and the history here.

Has that influx of new residents and visitors had a noticeable effect on the city itself?

Yeah, because with the storm, you had a lot of shops that were just suddenly closed down or abandoned, and they needed business owners. So, suddenly, you had a lot of opportunity here, and right now, the city is going through a boom period. The tourism market has grown, and we've even got Hollywood down here now, shooting a bunch of movies around parts of the city. Including a lot of the places that were basically left to rot after Katrina, like the old Six Flags theme park. Those locations tend to get used for, like, apocalyptic scenes. They were filming the new *Planet of the Apes* sequel here, two years ago. So, in kind of a weird way, you could say Katrina put New Orleans back on the map.

Earlier, you mentioned the warmer water in the Gulf of Mexico and how that plays an integral role in exacerbating hurricanes that are starting to form. This alone suggests that the overall warming of our environment is something that's very much on your radar. Thinking about this semantically...what does "climate change" mean to you?

Um...climate change...to me it's just the...unbalancing of the earth. From its natural weather patterns. It's not the weather itself. Weather is volatile. You don't know exactly what to expect. But climate is what keeps the earth kind of in sync. And we're messing that up. You can see it here in Louisiana, especially. The weather patterns are changing. We've had to deal more intense storms, colder winters. We get snow now! That never used to happen in New Orleans.

Can you tell me about the first time that you saw snow in New Orleans?

I was in high school. We were in math class, sitting at our desks, and then somebody screamed out, "Look at these white flakes falling from the sky!" And we were like, *"What is this?!"* It was so unnatural that, like, a centimeter of snow shut down the entire city. We were completely unprepared. To me, stuff like that...it's the earth trying to counteract all the things we're doing to it.

Do you expect that the scientific community's predictions of worsening weather will come true?

I do. I think it'll happen within our lifetime. Because between New Orleans and Baton Rouge is something we call "Cancer Alley." It has the most cancer-causing emissions of any part of the country, because of all the oil refineries there with these huge smokestacks, throwing all kinds of chemicals up into the air.[1] It wreaks havoc on the citizens of the small towns in that area. And nobody's really doing anything about it except paying off families when someone gets sick or some kind of contamination incident happens. The oil companies have so much cash they can pay off anyone, including politicians. So, to me, the entire political discussion around climate change...it's all a money game to me.

Do you see any positive steps being taken at all, to mitigate the effects of climate change or even just pollution on a local level?

Other than plans being proposed and public transportation being pushed harder by the city...no, not much. Probably the most significant step is that some of the electric companies here have been working with solar farms in Eastern New Orleans and parts of Mississippi. And while that definitely qualifies as change, it's not really big enough to feel like we're actually doing as much as we could do.

---

[1] Some studies have disputed the idea that the industry of "Cancer Alley" has led to higher cancer rates in the surrounding neighborhoods. However, the majority of these studies were conducted by local oil companies, most notably the Shell Oil Company.

Why do you think we can't seem to try harder?

I don't know why. Part of it is, just, lack of awareness in our communities. Everybody wants to pay two dollars a gallon for gas. Nobody really thinks about what truly goes into that two-dollar price tag.

How often do the likely implications of climate change enter your thoughts?

Um...I won't say on a daily basis, but, on days when you do have these unusual patterns coming in...where in one minute, it'll be bright and sunny, and in less than half an hour, it'll be pouring rain and windy, and then it'll be sunny again...that's when I think about it. So, I try to do my part in reducing the impact we're having on the climate. Things like being conscious of how much water I'm using, not leaving lights on or wasting electricity, using public transportation and my bike as much as possible. If my friends and I need to drive someplace, we carpool or take a cab. Uber is kind of a new thing in New Orleans. We have really strong cab unions here.

Do you think these eco-conscious efforts are practiced by a lot of other people in your community?

It kind of depends on the economics. Like, in a really poor neighborhood, people might not have their lights turned on all day. But is that because they're worried about the climate or because they can't afford to forget stuff like that? Same thing goes for using a lot of the greener products like light bulbs. Those are more expensive than the usual ones. I can't afford to buy all of those things on a regular basis. And when you look at wealthy communities, they leave their lights on all day. They're driving, like, the nicest cars that get nine miles per gallon. People really like to show off their affluence here in the South.

You mentioned the expense of green products. Overall, how affordable do you find leading a greener lifestyle to be?

I actually find it *more* economical than you might think. Like, from not driving or owning a car, I save a lot of money each year. Actually, the savings aspects helps me stick to the whole thing. It's nice to have money for a rainy day. But as far as putting solar panels on your roof and switching your water system, I could see that being unaffordable right now.

Would you like to do that some day?

Oh, absolutely! I actually tried to look up blueprints and cost estimates for green structures the other week. If you wrote me a check, I'd start searching for land tomorrow.

Overall, how does climate change affect your thoughts and plans for the future?

That's a good question. Well...um...when I'm not working on the Loyola campus—I work in the office of residential life at the school—I'm studying to get my pilot's license. I'm a part of AOPA which the Aircraft Owners and Pilots Association. So, I do take an interest in what new kinds of aeronautical technologies are being worked on. Like, Richard Branson, he's been funding research on green and renewable fuel alternatives for Virgin America, which could be a catalyst for change across the entire industry.[2]

Is New Orleans where you'd like to stay for the long term?

Yes. I love this city.

I know some people who've had to relocate due to weather trends. Not just on the Gulf Coast. Has anyone left your community permanently due to concerns about future storms and weather?

We actually talk about that a lot, my friends and I. And that's actually why I want to stay in New Orleans. Because as far as the hurricanes go, I can see where they're born. The worst thing that could happen to New Orleans would be if the eye of a hurricane came straight up through the mouth of

---

[2] Richard Branson is a member of The Breakthrough Coalition, a multinational group of investors who have fashioned themselves as advocates for public and private investment in renewable energy. Bill Gates and Mark Zuckerberg are members of the Coalition as well.

the Mississippi River. That would bring the storm surge up here, it would overpower the levies, and the damage would just be...unimaginable. The city couldn't recover from it.

Is it difficult to live with the possibility of that happening?

I try not to think about it. But, in the event that it did happen...I have a timeline, if I need to get out.

KEVIN & OLIVIA

25 and 24 years old
Church Administrators
Belchertown, Massachusetts

December 13, 2014

INTERIOR. A living room. The smell of chicken casserole is in the air. A small christmas tree lights up the room. Outside, there's darkness, wind, and lots of ice.

So how did the two of you end up coming to Western Massachusetts? If I recall from our earlier email phone correctly, you're both from very different locales.

KEVIN: Well, after spending most of my childhood in the Sacramento area, I was scouting around for schools, knowing that I wanted to study linguistics. A few years earlier, I had been in a hostel in San Francisco and discovered an old linguistics book in their library, and was like, "Oh. This is really cool." And so, when I looked around, I started including public universities. And the college that offered the best deal happened to be UMASS Amherst, all the way across the country. So I went from west coast to east coast.

OLIVIA: I grew up about two hours north of London, but my mum, she's American. She went to university in the states. And for my mum's tenth reunion, she brought me over here with her, and I fell in love with the campus of her school and the surrounding area. So, I ended up attending Mount Holyoke and have subsequently stayed in the area.

And what have you both been doing with your lives since that chance meeting that brought the two of you here?

KEVIN: After graduation, we got married. It was a July wedding. And we were trying to figure out what was next. And trying to decide whether we wanted to go back to England, or stay local, or go even further abroad somewhere. And...it just felt like God was really calling for us to stay local, here, in the states. We started talking with our church and they kept saying, "Hey, you guys should stick around" So from there, we talked about what the church was trying to accomplish, what our roles would be, and through that, now, I'm basically in a pastoral training position. So, I work partially with college students, meeting with them one-on-one, meeting with them on campus, planning outreach events. And I run a few community groups within our church. But, in addition, just to supplement the bills, I do research in a lab on campus. Cognitive linguistics. We do EEGs,[1] putting those nets on people's heads and measuring different brain stimuli. That's a lot of fun.

OLIVIA: So, I spend most of my time working for our church. My technical title is Administrative Associate but I the majority of the position consists of doing creative things, and that's what my day generally looks like. Either producing slides and graphics for church, for varying things that they

---

[1] EEG is an acronym for "Electroencephalogram." It is, as Kevin said, a hairnet comprised of metal censors that is placed on the head to measure brain wave patterns. In recent years, market research companies have begun using EEGs to measure how the human brain responds to advertisements.

need. Organizing events. Thinking about how we can improve the event planning process, structurally.

There have been a number of studies indicating that faith is in something of a decline with Millennials. A lot of them appear to be rejecting organized religion, or at least trailing away from it. What do you both see, being so close to a major college campus?

KEVIN: I guess, here, we interact with college students and I just see a lot of brokenness and apathy. People who just don't care. They don't have a purpose in life, they don't really know who they are. They don't know why they exist. And...they're just kinda lost and confused. I see that a lot, and I have conversations. And I ask, "What do you believe?" And they don't know. So that's something. I want people to have hope, a purpose, and identity. That's something that I try to help them find, through the church. Bringing people Jesus and showing them that there is hope. You are loved. Your life has meaning beyond yourself. You exist for a reason. Their life, their being here, isn't just a random chance. God actually loves them enough to have made them.

OLIVIA: I think for me, it would be of a very similar or identical vein. Working for a church and trying to be a minister to students, to people within the church. And really, being able to share the gospel. I feel that my role is less of a direct sharing with people and more like being an enabler who can make things happen, so that others can be more efficient in the way that they share or provide outreach to people in the area. Especially college students.

What is your church trying to accomplish here? What are you trying to accomplish?

KEVIN: The main thing I've wanted to see is unity. Bringing people together and fostering closeness. And so, I've been working with the different Christian groups on campus and trying to encourage working together. I organize and host these regional all-night prayer and worship nights, where we've got bands that just come and play for twelve hours straight. We invite churches from the area, and campus ministries...they come and lead the event for two hour slots. We've had lots of folks attend from the Brothers and Sisters in Christ, which is the main African-American Christian group on campus, to the Orthodox Christian Fellowship. And so, just seeing unity in that, it's almost like saying, "We're here for the same reason." We're here because of Jesus, and Jesus loves us enough—I mean, he died for us—and we're united in being able to show the world an alternative to this fractured thing where people are arguing over silly stuff that doesn't really matter.

How do you plan on performing this advocacy and outreach work in the near future? How do you reach and connect with students?

OLIVIA: We're planning a campus Mission Week right now. We're bringing in speakers from different ministry groups from places like Oxford, England, and Cambridge, right outside of Boston.

KEVIN: And they're gonna come together and deliver a full week of talks on campus. Lunch talks. Evening talks. Basically addressing really big picture questions.

OLIVIA: Starting from things as abstract as, "Is there truth? Is there justice? What do those even mean?" to "Is there a god? If there is a god, what kind of god is he? Can the bible be authenticated? Is it real? Who is Jesus?"

KEVIN: And then, also questions that are rooted in social justice issues. Like, "How can there be a god if there's also suffering?" The entire event is about trying to wrestle with those questions and answer them in the best way possible, and also showing people that Christianity isn't this silly thing for the ignorant and people who aren't educated. Some of the people who we're working with are PhDs doing top-level work in physics and biology, or history. And these people are like, "Yeah. I believe this. And I have years and years of research to prove it."

OLIVIA: Right. The entire week is a way showing people that Christianity is this legitimate thing and engaging with young people about that. Getting to the hard questions that are beneath any sort of religion. The things many people really want to know. "Who am I?" When people are asking if there is a god, what they're really getting at is, "Well, if there's a god, who am I?"

LEE

29 years old
Student
Holyoke, Massachusetts

December 19, 2014

INTERIOR. An old house on the edge of town, right next to a parking lot. Home repair tools and toys are everywhere. A chicken clucks from somewhere nearby. It's a cold and rainy night.

Let's begin with Holyoke. This is a part of Massachusetts most people never think of or experience. Tell me about your history with the city.

I grew up right around here. This is my home. This is the neighborhood I grew up in. I can't really picture myself living anywhere else. I love the river, nearby. I have a lot of memories of telling my parents I was going to the park and instead sneaking down to the river, finding bugs and stuff. There's a train track, like, parallel to the river. My friends, we'd climb up the hill and walk on the railroad tracks. And those tracks kinda lead you to anywhere around town. You can get to all kinds of destinations just by walking them. I always thought that was pretty cool.

Did you ever wonder about where else the tracks might lead and venture beyond the Connecticut River Valley?

Yeah. I spent about four years in Austin, Texas. We were living back up here beforehand—me, my husband, a friend, my sister and two year-old son, Billy—and we ended up losing our home. And we decided that the five of us were going to pack everything up, sell everything we couldn't carry, and go for a trip. We made most of our living as musicians, playing local shows, going on little music tours with other bands, and working service jobs when we need to. And that was our life for a while.

And now you've returned to Holyoke to attend college. What's your field of study?

Biology. The richness of the living. Everything here's just so alive. There's trees, plants, bugs...you look under a log and there's just so much to discover. I love that. And here, I don't get eaten by fire ants.

Where are you studying?

I'm a junior at the local state university. My major is sustainable food, farming, and entomology. I study insects. Something that gets me really excited about the direction the world is heading in is that there's all these little...there's Pinterest, there's Facebook, and I just see all these people trying to do things like growing a garden, or making medicine from plants they've grown. Foraging. Urban farming. Stuff like that just gets me really excited. I feel like the conversations about things that benefit the planet are shifting. In a good way.

How do you imagine taking some of the things you're learning at college and applying them to your life and community?

Something that really fascinates me is the idea of

living self-sufficiently, in a small scale way. A smaller chunk of land. Even...I'm constantly experimenting in my yard. Just trying to see what is possible on a smaller scale. Because that's more realistic for a majority of people on this planet. You know? Not everyone has a nice farm where they can raise every kind of crops and raise cows, pigs, whatever. And I think that deters a lot of people from trying to take a shot at this way of living. Part of what I want to do is be part of the research that's showing people that actually, you can have this self-sufficient lifestyle in a very small backyard or even a side lot. You can grow your own vegetables, keep a few chickens, whatever fits...save money, and...I dunno...be happy.

Holyoke has been through some very hard times as a city, economically. In spite of those struggles, do you see your interests in self-sufficiency and eco-friendly living reflected locally?

There are so many projects going on where I live. Having the river here is a big deal. People realize we need to keep it healthy and clean. There's a huge tree planting initiative happening right now. Not just here, but in neighboring towns. It's this idea, turning old industrial areas into green spaces. The goal is to plant more than 5,000 trees around here in the next year.

A lot of the young adults I've spoken with have expressed similar interest in sustainability and rebuilding when it comes to the environment.

Yeah. Absolutely. I get that. Here, we've got a really young political scene. Our mayor is 23 years old.[1] He's played a huge role in the tree-planting project, and I actually help out the non-profit that's managing the whole thing. It's a work-study job.

Having a young and active political scene in a small city like Holyoke is something of a distinction when you look at how young people are participating in elections on a national scale. Especially in the most recent round of midterm elections. Why do you think those voting metrics are so low when it comes to Millennials?

I just think that...I don't know. [laughs] I don't know. I'm sorry. It's a tough question to answer.

Indeed. That's why I'm doing all these interviews.

Well, I mean...I look at politicians and they're all middle-aged white men. They don't represent me, they don't represent the people I live with, in this town. We're 50% Puerto Rican. So many people here are in their 20s and 30s, and I just don't think that they're represented at all, naturally. You turn on the TV and it's all older white guys. And you can't trust them. There's so much, like...through

---

[1] Mayor Alex Morse, the Millennial-aged Mayor of Holyoke whom Lee referred to, won the job in 2012, defeating 67 year-old former Mayor Elaine A. Pluta. A similar Millennial Mayor upset recently occurred in Fall River, another economically troubled city in Massachusetts.

Facebook and all the social media...you see how much corruption there really is. It's now so easy to find that information just by going online. And it's so frustrating! It's like, "*Who do you trust?*" These days, I don't want to vote because I don't trust any of the people on the ballot. Not any of them.

What could these people do that might renew your faith in their commitment to being ethical and trustworthy public servants?

They would literally have to accept only small donations for their campaign. You know what I mean? It's not fair that some of these politicians are taking in millions of dollars from maybe one company...come on. They're not representing me. They're representing that company, their interests. Now, if the absolute contribution limit was, like, $1,000, I would be able to donate and feel like it actually meant something. I would be represented because my five dollars is the same as everyone else's five-dollar donations. It's more fair. They would be representing people, not corporations, or...rich people. [laughs]

JOSE & OWEN

24 and 27 years old
Teachers
Virginia Beach, Virginia

February 15, 2015

INTERIOR. A TGI Fridays restaurant. Laughter. Chicken wings. Pale ale. It's the aftermath of an intramural dodgeball match. The players are here.

Jose, tell me about your relationship to the Virginia Beach area.

JOSE: I grew up pretty much right here in Virginia Beach. Left for about four years. US Army service. For all my army guys out there... [gives fist pump]...and now I'm pretty much back here. Right now...I used to do a lot of MMA in the past, Mixed Martial Arts competitions, and right now I do one-on-one training with kids and teens in the area. That's what I've got going on right now, and also, Dodge ball Thursdays, man! Just to keep something going. Come out here, have a good time.

What does your MMA training involve these days? Are you gonna go home and pound out four hours of lifting and cardio after we finish these wings and this pitcher of Rolling Rock?

JOSE: Well, I've taken a bit of a break from the competitive scene, but not for long. Right now, my plan for getting back into fighting shape mainly involves nutrition. Here, I'm kind of splurging a bit right now, right? Nothing wrong with that. You gotta do it before you start hitting it hard. Then, come next week, it's game time. It's gonna be a lot of regimented eating. The right portions, the right combinations of carbohydrates, proteins, and healthy fats. I'm gonna be hitting the weights hard. And then, one year from now, you're gonna see a whole different me. Total transformation.

Ideally, what will you look like when that transformation is complete?

JOSE: Oh man. [laughs] Arnold Schwarzenegger, but a little bit better than that. And hotter.

Before dodge ball, when we were driving over, you said you want to channel your MMA training into opening a gym. A place where you can teach more regularly. What made you want to do that?

JOSE: I've always been inspired by the martial arts scene. As a youth, I used to watch all the Kung Fu movies, just like every other kid does. But this time, as an adult, it was just something I was really interested in. Self-defense, I think self-defense is very important for people to learn. It's a kind of independence. You know? So I said to myself, "I'm gonna learn everything there is to know about nutrition, martial arts in general, and then, one day, I will have my own gym." I couldn't have done it without the Internet. That was huge when I started doing my research.

Being able to defend yourself...what is it about that ability that's important to you? There's the independence angle, like you said, but does it run deeper than that?

JOSE: Absolutely. It's about being headstrong too.

You go out on the street, and sometimes you don't feel comfortable going down an alley or by a certain apartment. Or whatever. Sometimes, with kids, there's the issue of running into bullies. I want to teach people to feel confident in themselves. So then, that way, they can bring that and teach their children. If enough people approach martial arts like that, it becomes more than just fighting. It becomes about respecting yourself and one another. There are people who instruct and use these skills for absolutely the wrong reason, and that's not what I want to do. I want to turn something I love into a teaching platform that can bring out the best in people.

Owen, what about you? How far back do you and Virginia Beach go?

OWEN: These are my roots as well. I grew up less than a mile away from this bar. I moved to Blacksburg to attend Virginia Tech, studied automotive technology, and then went and worked for the industry for about six years. Then I came back here and started teaching at our local vocational high school. I teach automotive technology to freshmen.

Is that a tall order? How easy do you find it, working with students at that age? The challenges of being a teacher have been exhaustively documented.

OWEN: Sure. Trying to get students engaged, trying to get them excited about learning? That's my biggest challenge, and it's my number one goal. As far as what works...right now, my age is beneficial. I can make a stronger connection with the students than some of the older teachers can. I'm trying to work on a method that I can turn to when I get older, that'll still keep the students fired up. I'm learning as I go.

Is education on a national level an issue you find yourself preoccupied with?

OWEN: Sometimes, but the issues that really concern me right now...well, the first is trusting the government, trusting politicians. It's political contributions from big companies, people with a lot of money versus...me. I don't have a lot of money. I can only make a small contribution to a campaign. Does my voice really count? That's what it comes down to.

What's the second issue that you think about often?

OWEN: The environment. I think, the people who deny climate change...it's ignorant. We need to do something about it for future generations.

As an individual, what do you feel you can do about either of those issues?

OWEN: Just cutting down on energy consumption at home. If everyone makes a little effort, it can go along way. Transitioning to more fuel-efficient cars. That ties right into my automotive background. I definitely talk to my students about fuel economy. We've talked about hybrids, electric cars...I did some contract engineering research for Tesla motor company awhile back.

How about voting? We're coming right out of the midterms and it appears that Millennials largely stayed home. What do you think happened? Why didn't more people show up?

OWEN: I work with young people and what I hear...they feel that their vote is not going to count. A lot of my students, they're looking ahead at the first election they'll be able to vote in, and they're already saying, "I'm not gonna go out and vote. It's pointless." They don't realize that if they vote, and they get their friends to vote...well, it adds up.

JENNA & MARIAN

19 and 20 years old
Students
Ann Arbor, Michigan

March 28, 2015

EXTERIOR. The entryway to a dining hall. The end of lunch rush. Students course across the common. The air is crisp. The sky is bright blue.

What brought you both to Ann Arbor and the University of Michigan?

JENNA: I grew up in an area of Minnesota that was pretty conservative, and so, I think I was just ready for something new and very different. One thing I was really interested in was how socially conscious and active a lot of the college scene seems to be these days. It seems like a lot of students here are interested in social justice and are very aware. It's almost like a new normal. And that was something I really, really wanted to be surrounded by.

MARIAN: Same here. What I'm studying right now is German studies, which doesn't really have much to do with what my passions are. Honestly, I'm studying German studies mainly because it was the major that was easiest to finish the fastest, so that I can devote more time to my job as an organizer, which has to do with animal issues, which is what I care about. So, I try to do some sort of action or event every week that involves animal issues. This Sunday, I'll be doing a demonstration with some people at the regional airport. We'll be protesting Delta. Air France is their partner, and Air France transports live beagles and primates to their deaths in labs.

What's keeping you engaged at school if your principal

interests are beyond the campus?

MARIAN: The degree. It's basically a prerequisite for a job you can support yourself with.

How did animal rights become the driving issue that mattered to you?

MARIAN: It has to do with my family. I was raised meatless. My parents both sort of came to that on their own. But then after they came to that, it became a thing for our family. I became a vegan later, on my own, because I sort of bought into this myth you hear in elementary school. You know, milk is just produced by cows eating grass and they need to be milked because it hurts them. But when I realized that the milk industry is actually really messed up, and that it's pretty much married to veal production, that's when I became a vegan. And then my parents started to adjust their own diet to something closer to veganism. So, I think that the views you inherit from your parents...you have to decide how well they apply to the world you inherit.

And Jenna, is there any particular issue that stood out to you at an earlier age? For similar experiential reasons?

JENNA: I think I've always struggled with, like, choosing a priority issue. In high school, my main issue of importance was probably LGBTQ issues and equality. I was pretty active with my school's GSA [Gay-Straight Alliance] and right now, I've been getting a lot more into animal rights issues and also just environmental issues, as a whole. I mean, I've always been generally interested in those things, but I never had a network or a group to, uh...to pursue that. But now, here, at college, I feel like I've found that.

Was this the first time when you truly felt you had a support network that cared about these causes that are near and dear to you?

JENNA: Um...I was in tenth grade when I joined the GSA and I think being in that group, before college, was a start because even though the group was more of a support network than an outreach group, I was able to learn so much about the supportive presence of different people and their interest in the queer community. I didn't have any real information source about that community until then, so that was a really eye-opening experience. And later in high school, I did get more involved in the leadership of the GSA. That helped me feel more informed and to feel responsible for educating myself about the issue and educating others. Which is what I'm trying to do right now, right here.

Marian, how about you? Was there much of a support network for you where you grew up? Did you feel isolated as someone concerned with animal issues?

MARIAN: I was definitely not normal, in that way. I mean, I started out in elementary school being the only kid who was vegetarian. People thought that was weird and that my parents were somehow abusing me by raising me without meat. And until college, that was pretty standard. I had to leave Arizona before I found an environment where other people were open to the idea that some lifestyles are better for the environment, that animals don't deserve to be tortured, that vegetables are healthy.

JENNA: There's a lot more awareness here, about a lot of issues. So much that now, I've been trying to think of ways to branch out more and pursue activism outside of campus.

That's something I often wonder about college activism. How easily it can expand beyond campus and potentially shape public policy? And it brings up something that I can't help but see as a paradox. Today, we've got more and more college students, like yourselves, who care about major issues and want to play to a role in addressing them. And yet, most students and other people our age barely voted in the last midterm elections this year. Why do you think that is? In theory, voting is the easiest way for any concerned citizen to make a difference.

JENNA: Hmm...I think, possibly, one reason why young people aren't voting would be...not seeing ourselves represented in the political realm. Not really identifying with politicians, their age, gender, background. Or not really thinking...not feeling as much like a part of the system. Or maybe feeling like it's our job to make change outside of that system?

MARIAN: Yeah. After college, thinking about what I'll do at that point, I have this vision of me and my cousin living together in Norfolk, Virginia and working for PETA, from their headquarters. Bringing animal issues to new generations of people. I think, at least locally, that would make a bigger difference.

ALEX & VERONICA

21 and 22 years old
Students
Nashville, Tennessee

May 18, 2015

INTERIOR. A student apartment. The futon has been set up. It's well after midnight. Three bottles of dark beer occupy the kitchen table.

Each of you, tell me a little bit about what you're studying here at Tennessee State and what led you to that field.

ALEX: I'm studying a kinesiology. I thought I wanted to do physical therapy because I was in physical therapy a bunch during high school for a leg injury. But I realized I was interested in this field for the wrong reasons: it was a "good" job and it would pay a lot of money. Now I'm a lot more intrigued by the nutritional side of health management, and I plan on taking my work and studies in a more holistic direction in the near future.

VERONICA: That's kind of like the path I went down. I did my first year of undergrad at Union University in Jackson. I decided to study nursing because it would help people, but also because it was a steady, paying job. But over time, I realized I didn't want to do just that. So I started taking public health classes and that's what I'm now studying here at Tennessee State. And I'm trying to combine it with courses that touch on sustainable food and farming.

When the two of you look beyond campus, at issues bigger than your current academic careers, what's something that concerns you?

ALEX: Something that really concerns me—and something that I actually want to spend much of my life working towards fixing—is the problem of people not exercising and eating healthy. One of my professors often says that the cheapest and most effective medicine is exercise. It's literally free, and it works. But it can be hard for people to actually get down to it.

VERONICA: Yeah, and I think consumerism plays a big part in that discouragement. I mean, you never see an advertisement for something so simple as an apple. That's not something that you can market, as opposed to complex exercise products. I don't think our current system really allows much space for boiling exercise down to the basics, even though I one hundred percent agree with you, Alex.

ALEX: And that's the problem! "The Man." [laughs]

VERONICA: Fuck The Man. [laughs] I don't say that in an angsty way. It's very realistic.

ALEX [to Veronica]: What about you? What's your issue?

VERONICA: Climate change. Because even if we're addressing all of these human challenges, if the temperature of the earth rises by just a few degrees Celsius, none of that matters because we're all dead. In order to sustain any dialogue about how to uplift humanity, we also need to be here. You know? But I'm also a bit torn over the whole thing. It's a lot easier to engage with helping people directly, whereas climate change is this enormous issue that's been slowly getting worse for decades and it can be tougher to find a way to approach that type of issue as an individual.

So then, thinking of serious issues like these, what do you two feel you'll be able do to address those issues once you're finished with college? Or even right now?

VERONICA: Well, you know the whole idea of being carbon neutral? There's this guy named Daniel Greenberg who's basically saying, "Neutral isn't good enough. We need to restore ecosystems, instead of just preserving them." So he has a company called Earth Deeds and he's doing something called "onsetting." He gets companies to put a price on the carbon that they emit. Then, the companies and clients join forces to literally pay for those emissions. The money goes to the local government, which takes that money and invests it in environmental projects, like, setting up solar panels someplace. That's a really effective way to tackle the climate change issue, and it's something I definitely think about on a personal level.

ALEX: Right, and I think one of the problems that young and generally aware people face is that there are actually so many ways to positively address a big issue: far more than the ones we immediately perceive. In terms of climate change, you know, there's changing the light bulbs in your house, and then there's something more big picture like the onsetting approach. There just seems to be a limit to what perceived risks people are willing to take, in tackling the things they care about.

One of the oldest and safest ways for people to add their voices to a national or global issue is voting. But lately, in America, a lot of people in the 20-something age range haven't been turning up for midterm and local elections. Why do you both think that's happening now?

VERONICA: I remember, someone I know once posed the question, "If voting actually made a difference, don't you think the government would have found a way to stop it by now?"

ALEX: Someone said that about the American government?

VERONICA: Yeah, it just a snarky aside, but still.

ALEX: Well…[sighs] I don't know. I mean, voting is important, but sometimes I can't get over the thought that my one vote doesn't really matter. And when a large portion of people in our generation aren't voting, that's a problem. I think general laziness is part of that problem, but what I think it comes down to—for me, at least—is when I think of voting, I can also think of so many things I could do with my day, like volunteering or just talking with people, that would have a greater and more noticeable impact on the lives of people in my community.

VERONICA: It would be interesting if there was some sort of an online community that could generate constant dialogue on specific ballot questions and candidates, in a much more straightforward way than what we see on TV news or even online media sites. Just to keep the passion of voting alive. There's probably already a platform for that, but it would neat if it could somehow override the usual information channels we use. Because it's really hard to get a sense of what so many politicians actually stand for these days, when you compare campaign promises that some of these politicians make with what they actually do once elected.

ALEX: Right. To actually vote on something in an informed and responsible way requires a ton of research beyond what you see on the news or read on campaign flyers. And even if doing that research is something that we would categorize as every voter's responsibility, I don't know if it's realistic—with the pace of life and the economic demands these days—to assume that every American is actually going to do their homework before voting. Or vote at all.

WESLEY

32 years old
Unemployed
Tallahassee, Florida

August 21, 2015

EXTERIOR. A strip mall parking lot. Evening. Dark clouds rumble overhead. The lights of small businesses cast an eerie glow across the concrete.

The question of how to get involved in politics, even on a local level, can be mystifying for a lot of people. Tell me about your formative experience.

My first political experience with politics...I was 19 years old and volunteering on a campaign for our incumbent congressman. After that, I volunteered for a few more campaigns, interned for Howard Dean in New Hampshire in 2004, which was my first full-time experience. And by "full-time," I mean 70-75 hours a week. Or more. Then I started handling staffing tasks for local campaigns. Eventually came to manage two of them, both for state offices. And then...uh...I've kinda called it quits for now.

What made you decide bow out?

I needed to catch up on sleep. [laughs] Campaign work doesn't leave room for much of a life.

Indeed. Campaign work is notoriously time-consuming and grueling. What compelled you to devote years of your life to such a demanding occupation?

It may sound silly but the way that I first got involved with political stuff was through student government, in college. We had a big parking problem in our residential area and I got involved with the student government to try and solve it. We ended up reaching a resolution with the parking services folks on campus and I thought, "Wow. You can actually get involved and accomplish something." So, uh, from there...I started looking at real world politics, on a state level.

When you look at real world politics today, is there a single issue—or a set of issues—that strikes you as particularly urgent? What do you feel we should be addressing right now, on a local level and beyond?

Well, the biggest issue that's playing into politics these days is the overwhelming, corrupting influence of money in politics. It's not necessarily old school corruption, like, I bring you a suitcase full of money in exchange for you hooking me up with a vote on the floor of Congress or something. But it's more systemic. It's about who has access to lawmakers, the decision makers. And it's more and more skewing towards the wealthiest in our country, who have that kind of access and can do what they want. And the ability to do what you want, quite frankly, is power.

Have you been able to play a role in the growing efforts to initiate some sort of campaign finance reform and get big money out of politics?

Yeah, I have. The organization I was working for most recently, their focus was campaign finance reform and political corruption. We did a lot of outreach and working with volunteers, and we decided to do a pilot project. Since...well, nothing is moving at the Congressional level and it's almost as hard to pass things at the state level...so we decided to focus locally. And we ran a ballot question in Tallahassee that would basically lower the amount of money that could be contributed to candidates. Put an ethics watchdog on the electoral process. And provide some sort of citizen-funded campaign finance fund. So, we won there, with a 2-1 ratio, which is pretty satisfying, and now the organization that I worked for is looking to push this in other cities and even at a state level.

So you're in the weeds, tackling an issue that's profoundly determining who has the most influence in our political system. And it's an issue that a lot of Americans feel strongly about. There are studies and polls that strongly suggest that most Americans support campaign finance reform. The kind of reform your organization was trying to bring about locally. When you told people about what you were working on, how did they react?

That's a really good question, and for the duration of the time I was working with this organization on getting big money out of politics, I would explain it to people and their reaction was instantly, "Good luck with that." You know, with a sarcastic tone. Because everybody...90 percent of people want to see some sort of reform on the issue, but probably about 90 percent of people think there's nothing that can be done about it. So, it's really a matter of getting a couple of small victories—mostly local, where people can impact policy the most—in order to say, "Yes, we can actually do this." And then bumping it up to higher levels, like, statewide ballot questions, for example. And then eventually taking the push to Congress, where it's probably most needed.

A lot of people feel like change needs to happen right now, in a very noticeable way. Is it easy for you to stay motivated when change comes at a slower and more incremental rate?

Yeah, I'd say so. I'd say that people taking a look at any victory...at the organization, we said that one of the biggest motivations is just having one victory under your belt. People see that. You don't want to work for a losing candidate or cause. But when you see that there's progress being made and you're chipping away at it, bit by bit, people want to jump on that.

So what's next for you, with this political organizing experience under your belt?

That's a funny question because I'm actively seeking other places to live and work right now. I plan to do a little bit of traveling to escape what's going to turn into another very rainy fall and see some other places where I might want to live.

What are the top contenders thus far?

So, uh, the ideal picks are a couple places in California. The Sacramento area. Santa Cruz, if I could afford the housing there. San Diego. Denver is also up there. And Salt Lake City. A couple of those places are really adept at ballot question work. California and Colorado both have questions on their ballots almost every single election cycle. So, people are used to taking politics into their own hands instead of just leaving it to legislators.

Well, wherever you end up, I'm sure it'll be interesting to see how engaged your peers are, on the local issues. That's something I'm rather concerned about. The exit polls from this year's midterm election—which is basically a marathon of local elections—were pretty dismal. Why do you think that happened? It's not the first time. Millennials have been somewhat lethargic in their election day efforts, even during the presidential races. Why aren't we as involved as our parents and grandparents?

I think for a lot of young people, it's that they're, uh, not yet paying property taxes, which is one reason why people would pay attention to local politics, especially. Maybe...they just don't feel like the system is actually working for them? I know that's the case with a lot of people under the age of 30. The idea that it's all kind of a futile effort. For a lot of people, it's that they do move around so often. When you're not in one particular place, it's a little bit harder for you to get established and understand what's going on around you. It's tough to meet with your local lawmakers and develop a rapport with other political influencers. I mean, I've moved about once each year for the last 15 years. And it's about to happen again.

DANI

26 years old
Student
Los Angeles, California

June 17, 2015

EXTERIOR. A residential street. Lots of sun. Palms provide what little shade there is. The buzz of a police helicopter echoes across the sky. Very LA.

You're a native Californian. Has the southern half always been home?

I've lived in LA my whole life. Grew up in the valley,[1] but I just moved here to Palms[2] because it's where I need to be to get to school in the mornings.

So, give how well you know this city, these landscapes, everything about the area...SoCal has been in a severe drought for over a year now. I'm curious, how visible is that drought to you?

Well, it's not something I think about on a day-to-day basis, which is pretty bad. I mean, if I'm taking a shower or doing something that requires water, I'll remember. When I have the opportunity to not waste water, I'll try not to, but it's not like I actively go out of my way to do research on the drought and what it might mean for the future. It's not like I can solve the problem

---

[1] "The valley" is LA shorthand for the San Fernando Valley: a sprawl of suburbs and industry to the northwest of central Los Angeles. It's home to nearly 1.8 million people.

[2] Palms is a neighborhood in west Los Angeles that young residents have flocked to in recent years due to relatively affordable housing prices. LA is becoming a very expensive place in which to live.

myself.

When did you first hear about the drought in a way that made its severity register with you?

I think I first heard about it during the Ice Bucket Challenge,[3] that thing where people dumped buckets of ice water on their heads and posted videos of the whole thing on Facebook to, like, raise awareness for some disease. I can't remember which one. And after watching some of the videos, I saw a bunch of people commenting that there was a drought going on in California while people were doing this, and I thought, "Well, that's a stupid thing to do." So I didn't do the Ice Bucket Challenge. That was when the drought registered for me, and really, it was all thanks to social media.

There seems to be an "everyone doing their part" mentality in certain LA neighborhoods I've been to. How easy is it for you to find ways to conserve water in your day-to-day life?

I try to do bigger loads of laundry instead of a bunch of small loads. My building is having all the residents conserve water by limiting the laundry room to only one washing machine. I don't know if that's because they're worried about the drought

---

[3] The Ice Bucket Challenge was a 2014 social media event in which participants chose between publicly donating money to Lou Gehrig's Disease research groups or sharing a video of themselves dumping ice water over their heads and encouraging their friends to make donations.

or because they're just fucking cheap, but...you know. It does create some squabbles between neighbors. But my boyfriend and I, we just throw everything in and fill the machine as high as we can. We also try to let our dishes pile up until there's enough to fill the dishwasher, because I think doing every item by hand under the faucet wastes more water. I've stopped showering everyday. Now I only do it whenever I get sweaty or start to smell. One of the things I think ladies can do, like...when you're shaving your legs or lathering up, you don't need to have the water running the entire time. Just turn it off, do your business, and then, rinse off. Simple. Done. When it comes to oral hygiene, I used to use one of those water picks that shoots out water to clean between your gums, and I've stopped running it since the drought began. So, in not using it and letting my teeth get worse, I have been conserving water. [pause] You're welcome, LA.

How do you think a lot of people here would respond upon hearing about your approach?

They'd probably tell me I'm gross. I don't know. People get really weird sometimes, when I tell them I'm showering less because of the drought. A lot of people here shower multiple times a day. You know LA. People are obsessed with how they look. I mean, that's not to say I don't care, but some days I don't need to wash off. I mean, at the very least, I'll skip washing my hair sometimes.

Is this something you talk about with your friends and colleagues? Do you all swap ideas for everyday water conservation?

I haven't really talked to my friends about it. The ones who are in school right now, they're mostly just concerned with studying. They don't really care about wasting water. The only place where I really see the drought being talked about regularly is on social media. Less now, though. I think the online conversation has actually died down lately. I did see an article recently about people's lawns and how you don't need to have a lawn to be happy and how there are all these people in Beverly Hills right now refusing to stop watering their lawns. And, you know, they've got tons and tons of land that has to be watered to stay green. And that makes me wonder, "If I'm conserving all this water in my everyday life, who am I conserving it for? Some fucker who's gonna sprinkle his estate?"

Do you see that casual wasting of water locally?

Not around here so much. But then again, this neighborhood is mostly apartment buildings. People don't really have lawns to get invested in. Go to a more residential area with houses and yeah, you'll see a lot of people out in the front yard with the garden hoses running.

Well, lawns are a huge part of the dream life here in LA. Take that away and a lot of people will feel like there's

this hole in the fabric of their existence. I know that
sounds ridiculous, but that sort of entitlement is decades
in the making.

I don't think letting your lawn die has to be a sacrifice. You can get creative on the home front. One thing I've had fun with lately is taking a water-less approach to gardening. Like...I was able to get a big box of clear plastic beads at this craft store nearby for, like, five bucks. And I used a glue gun to attach them to a bunch of bare branches I had in this vase. So in the right light, the beads look almost like dewdrops.

Then there's real plants. Succulents are huge now. You see a lot of succulents in pots, around storefronts and people's windows. It's becoming more fashionable, I guess. Kinda trendy. My boyfriend and I have kept a few little cactuses this year. We've got one that we kept alive for almost two years. I gave him the cactus at the beginning of our relationship, and it started growing, but now...um...this is what happened to it.

It was supposed to symbolize our love. It was our love cactus. Like, as long as the cactus stays alive, we'll be together. But now...it's kinda...it's...I don't know, it just looks like a bunch of floppy dicks hanging over the edge of a jar. Maybe that's what love is.

A bunch of floppy dicks hanging over the edge of a jar?

Yeah. Maybe that's what it's trying to tell us. But, anyway, that's eco-gardening.

When you and your boyfriend think of the future, of your shared future, how does the water issue influence those thoughts, if at all? No one knows how long this drought will last. How often do you think about the long-term consequences?

I mean...I'm really hoping that the scientists and the politicians and the planners who are actually trying to figure out a solution...I hope something comes together. I'm doing my part here, but that's nowhere close to a solution. Most of the water used out here goes into food production, so, as much as I'd like to think all these little tweaks I'm making in my lifestyle are making a difference, I really have no idea. If it gets to the point where I can't turn on my faucet and have a drink of water whenever I want, then yeah, I'll be thinking about it a lot more. Or I'll just move.

I'm hoping by the time it gets that bad I'll be dead and won't have to deal with it. But that's bad for everyone else.

So you do think it's going to get worse.

Definitely. As of now it seems like that's gonna happen. Maybe by then we'll have figured out how to do things like re-filter wastewater or take the salt out of sea water for drinking. I hope so. It feels like we're overdue for figuring those things out.

But yeah, I've seen these photos of reservoirs and lakes around the LA area and each year, they've been more and more dried up. That's pretty scary. And I'm like, "How did this happen? How could we not have *planned* for something like this happening?"

Why do you think we haven't planned for something like this?

I have no idea! Like...I mean, I'm not...I wasn't very conscious of water usage before all of this. I didn't think about it much at all....until I suddenly had to. You know?

"How does your student loan debt make you feel?

Tell us in 3 emojis or less."

Hillary Clinton
August 12, 2015

ARTHUR

34 years old
Product Manager
Seattle, Washington

June 15, 2016

INTERIOR. A busy street packed with small restaurants. Midsummer. It's unseasonably hot. The 9-to-5 crowd is walking and biking to lunch.

When did politics become something that you actively participated in?

I really wasn't very active, politically, until I was 18 and I was able to vote. I guess politics has always been on my mind because I'm gay, and that's, like, a personal issue for me, and just being gay is still very political. Before I was eligible to vote, I knew how gay people were being treated in this country and I knew that it would take a lot of political effort to secure change for LGBT people.

Tell me about the neighborhood you were raised in. What was the local political climate like?

I grew up in New York City, in Queens. My parents are first generation Korean-Americans. Our old neighborhood has become very, very Asian. [laughs] A lot of Chinese and Korean immigrants have settled there. My parents were never too involved in politics. I think they're somewhere between Independents and Republicans. Depending on the election cycle. Where I grew up, it was pretty Democratic, but I don't think most people in my immediate neighborhood were very consistently involved in politics. Most of them were working too much.

How about you? What was going on in your life when

you turned 18 and became eligible to vote? Were you working? In school?

Well, the first time I voted was in 2000, during my undergrad years at college. It was the original Bush vs. Gore race. So, it was awhile before I was able to vote for an actual winning president. [laughs] And I would call that period a pretty dark time. As my first political act, the whole thing was really seared into my memory, and it was kind of a weird feeling because I voted, and then I felt like...not only did *my* vote not matter, but nearly half the votes in the whole country didn't matter. Especially when the Supreme Court called the election in favor of Bush, when there were clearly issues with the voting totals from Florida. I mean, sure, depending on where you live, your vote can absolutely matter, but in that case...

I've been hearing this sentiment from a lot of young adults. The idea that their votes don't matter very much. Tell me more about how it felt voting in your first election and getting your ass kicked. Did it discourage you or embolden you?

In a lot of ways, it strengthened my resolve to vote and be politically active. It made me really, really angry! And I maintained that anger until the 2004 election, and from that point...I mean, that election was slightly less controversial. Kerry vs. Bush, no big fiasco with ballots. But even so, after that election, I felt even more defeated. Beforehand, you could at least think, "Well, the 2000 election was stolen for Bush." And he had four years to prove himself. But by 2004, he'd confirmed my worst assumptions, and half the country was idiotic enough to vote for him for a second term. Knowing that he won without cheating made me feel pretty despondent. And frightened.

Knowing that your vote was shot down because your concerns and values were apparently opposed by a majority of voters in this country, how did you handle that despondency? Did it affect your participation in politics? I ask because right now, Millennials are officially the largest living generation in this country, and what we're seeing with Trump, whose supporters are mostly Baby Boomers...this could very well be a sort of "last stand" for the values that overrode yours in 2004.

Maybe *the* last stand. [laughs] So, in 2004, I had started attending law school. When I decided to apply, I wanted to be involved in some kind of civil rights or social justice field. Advocacy. Or even...before deciding to go to law school, I had been thinking about trying to get a job working with EMILY's List, which is an organization that helps elect Democratic pro-choice women. But honestly, after 2004, my interest in political activism was shaken. It can be draining for your psyche, being so personally involved in these issues and then getting defeated again and again. When Bush won his second term, a part of me did give up a little bit.

Did the "Yes We Can"[1] upswing in 2008 with Obama and Biden running on a platform of liberal values make you feel more optimistic?

It did, it definitely did. But in some ways, I also felt like I had missed the boat. Because the change was so fast and drastic—compared to the Bush years—that it made my head spin. I couldn't figure out how some of the same people who decided to vote for Bush, twice, were now willing to vote for our first African-American president, whose full name is "Barack Hussein Obama." [laughs] It almost felt like my chance to "involved" in the Obama movement had passed, in certain respects.

Do you mean you felt like you had missed that moment when you're young—I mean, you're still young, but when you can become a part of a history-making movement that defines your youth? The way that the Vietnam War protests or the Civil Rights Movement defined youth for a lot of Millennials' parents?

Exactly. When I say I missed my chance to canvas or sign up people to vote, I mean, at that point in my life, I had become a corporate slave. I was working crazy, crazy hours at big corporate law firm here in Seattle. The election didn't really coincide with a good time in my life, when I could have been more involved. If I had been in college or even law school when it was happening, things could have been very different.

---

[1] "Yes We Can" was a principal slogan from Barack Obama's 2008 presidential campaign.

I've heard that lamentation about becoming less involved from a lot of folks who've entered the professional class. In some cases, it's not for lack of time but something else that's changed, internally.

Yeah, and I think as you get older, in general, you become less idealistic. A lot of kids grow up with the belief that they can change the world, and I mean, you *can*, but...the probability is overstated, to put it lightly.

That's a common critique of the Millennial generation. Special snowflake syndrome. We were brought up believing we were precious and could change the world. But believing that you can change the world does signal an interest in fixing big, systemic problems. Your burgeoning interest in "social justice" type issues is reflective of this. When did this become a fixation for you?

I think during the undergrad years. I was attending college on the west coast and it was a very liberal campus environment. I wouldn't say it was "political," but...there was a huge interest in not only advocating for minorities but educating the student body about issues pertaining to minorities. There was a black student association, an Asian-American student association, LGBT student association, a women's union. I guess through exposure and involvement with some of those organizations, I learned a lot about the political climate in this country, at the time.

When it came to primaries and elections, did you get the sense that your peers were active, or did that political energy tend to stay on campus?

For the most part, the energy didn't leave the campus that much. I think it's complicated. College is a little bubble, it's kind of a breeding ground. Something like 95% of my fellow students chose to live on campus, even through senior year. The only thing I can really recall doing outside of campus was...there was a march against the invasion of Iraq. Some students organized it and I participated. I also remember some smaller acts of local activism that students got involved with, like getting dining hall workers unionized.

Lots of people have said they feel that the more meaningful thing they can do is focus on smaller local issues. And I think regardless of one's stance on voting, there's something to be said for the efficacy of aiming small and seeing what happens next. Have you seen that attitude manifest itself among your friends and colleagues here in Seattle?

Absolutely. I agree with it. When you're looking at a question like, "How can I make sure *Roe v. Wade* isn't overturned?" there's very little you as an individual can do, or even an individual Senator or the president. If you focus on the small local issues, it's easier to get involved meaningfully and see your efforts at work. But in terms of anything I've done in Seattle, I have not been very politically involved, unfortunately. After law school, my political involvement pretty much tapered off or just stopped. Partly because of the political climate, but also because reality set in. Student loan obligations, mainly.

What were your next steps after law school, professionally?

I found an associateship position with the corporate law firm I mentioned earlier, and for economic reasons, it was very difficult to turn it down. And after that, I ended up working for the firm for...like...a very, very long time. [laughs] About eight years. And then, last fall, I changed careers and ended up working at a clean technology startup. Part of it was trying to do something that I felt mattered more. I'd be lying if I said, "Oh, I realized I wanted to be involved in environmental issues," but on a general level, I wanted to do something that would have a more positive impact on the world. And the environmental stuff just stood out the most.

Indeed. It's definitely the most commonly cited issue I've heard young adults talk about, across political lines. It might be a partisan issue for the country, but for Millennials...how does this particular issue strike you as an ideal outlet for making a difference?

Well, the climate issue is a classic example of something where everyone can have an impact. Local government is very effective at making changes on climate and energy policy. Right here, we've banned plastic bags and we're trying to make building codes more energy efficient. And really, everyone should be involved with this issue because it's, like, an extinction-level event. The best time to get involved was 20 years ago. The second best time is now. It's a practical self-preservation issue.

We hear the word "practical" a lot in this election. It has different meanings, depending on whom you ask. Or what generation you're talking to. I'd imagine most Millennials care about addressing climate change because we're going to be around long enough to deal with the probable consequences.

Right, and I think that's why we're seeing so many young people gathering around this cause. It's self-interest, but pretty vital too. You know?

I want to go back to your earlier comment about the Obama insurgency being head-spinning. That was another instance of young people gathering around a cause, around a person who was a champion of causes they believed in. Vocally, at least. Now it feels like we're entering a new kind of head-spin territory with this election and the Trump insurgency, which, of course, is not something most Millennials are rallying around. It feels like a primal reaction to the Obama years. People who voted for Trump during the primary-

Or people who voted for Bernie and are now considering voting for Trump. [shakes head] I think it's very interesting. I don't think the hardcore Trump supporters are indicative of most people. There will be some diehards and defectors on both sides, but it still seems like Independents will decide this election. Most people are gonna vote Republican or Democrat no matter what happens. It's this Independent sliver that decides things.

And yet, "sliver" might not be the right word anymore. As far as political registration goes, Independents are now the largest voting demographic in the nation. It's about 42% of the electorate at this point.[2]

Sure, but I don't think they're truly independent. I'd imagine a lot of people register as Independents so they can vote in both primaries or even just feel freer. But if 42% of the country was truly Independent in a committed way, I don't think we'd have a two-party system anymore. Or we shouldn't. [laughs]

How do you feel about this election?

I'm, like, more despondent than I was back in 2004. I feel that...as scared and enraged at Bush as I was, I would take him any day of the week over Trump being president.

What is it about Trump that horrifies you the most?

---

[2] This figure comes from a 2015 Gallup study.

Again, I think it's a potential extinction-level event. [laughs] And I don't think that's really exaggerating much. I feel it's his pure irrationality and egomania. Obviously I disagree with him on pretty much every single issue, like, building a wall around Mexico, or deporting Muslim-Americans. But with that kind of stuff, I really don't think he's that different from Ted Cruz or any of the far-right Republicans. People like Cruz are at least rational enough not to launch us into something catastrophic over a stupid issue. What really scares me about Trump is, I don't think he's really in the race because he cares about making America great again. I think he's doing it as an ego trip. *Nyah, nyah, nyah, I have absolutely no political experience and I can become President of the United States. Bite me.* Just another thing on his resume. It's an attention-seeking move. And...what I meant by "extinction-level event" was, his ego seems so fragile. It's like he's driven by rage and emotion. Nothing else. And if you have him, in combination with Kim Jong Un, another egomaniac...both have access to nuclear weapons. Eventually, one is gonna say that the other one has a small penis. And then it's World War III.

People have predicted that Trump's braggadocio would be his undoing somewhere during the primary, but it hasn't done derailed him. His supporters seem to love that bombast and vainglorious attitude. What's your take on why this works for Trump?

He's a master entertainer. People like to be thrilled

and they're kind of stupefied by his charisma and unlikely success. I think a lot of people are taking in the election like a reality TV show and Trump is...he's great at getting ratings. He succeeds by getting the biggest rise out of people. And...I don't know. Clearly, there are a lot more racist xenophobes out there than I thought.

Obama's victory made it seem like those sentiments were in recession. Though they've always been with us. Is the success of Trump's campaign surprising to you?

Yes and no. Like you said, racism and bigotry have always been with us, and there's usually a backlash to any sort of change, like Obama's victory. But the intensity of the comeback has been startling. Though I think there's a silver lining to it. Now it's like, the devil is out there, and you know who's racist or homophobic among the people you know because they're less shy about it.

This has been a really toxic election season. The grim rhetoric on the right, the infighting on the left. Does any of this bile bubble up to the surface when you're with your friends and acquaintances?

I mean, I definitely live in a bubble. I have very few Republican friends, and the ones who are...maybe I'm wrong, but I don't think they're going to vote for Trump. They're in favor of marriage equality, which is key because if they weren't, I couldn't be friends with them. My boyfriend is the opposite. He can still be friends

184

with someone opposed to certain LGBT rights if they connect over other issues. I can't do that. But I think that what I experience most, in my circle, is #BernieOrBust[3] people who are mad about Hillary Clinton winning the Democratic nomination and would rather write in "Bernie" or vote for Jill Stein. And I just try to avoid getting involved. I read the Facebook comments, see the Likes, and I just roll my eyes.

What do you think youth participation in this election is going to look like? Obviously, you're in a bubble, but talking to your friends, do you get the sense that people are looking forward to voting for the next president?

I don't think so, and that's unfortunate. The sense I have is that youth participation peaked with Obama. But even then, it wasn't, like, gangbusters.[4] The media narrative at the time carried so much energy. *"The youth are the ones who will deliver the election to Obama."* That's what I remember hearing, over and over. And the youth definitely helped, but I don't know if it was a make-or-break kind of thing. So, right now, I get the sense that young people aren't fired up about Clinton nearly as much as they were for Obama, and that their fear of Trump isn't strong enough to compensate

---

[3] #BernieOrBust is a hashtag used by voters who supported Bernie Sanders during the 2016 Democratic Primary and have vowed to write in "Bernie Sanders" on their ballots rather than vote for challenger Hillary Clinton, who won the primary.

[4] Most studies estimate that roughly 53% of Millennial-aged Americans voted in 2008. I would agree with Arthur. "Gangbusters" seems an overstatement.

for that lack of enthusiasm. I would guess that unless there's an enormous effort to get out the vote, youth participation in this election will be lower than it was in 2008 or 2012.

Speaking as a Millennial, why do you think our apparent disinterest in voting persists? This has happened with prior generations, including Boomers, but we seem to be riding that wave of apathy and pessimism for a longer duration.

I think Millennials have been taught to become distracted by things that absolutely do not matter. [laughs] It's like, society-wide brainwashing. People will wait in line for 12 hours to get the newest iPhone, but they won't wait 10 minutes to vote. I mean, there are definitely voting problems throughout this country in which a long wait time could be a deterrent. I don't mean to rag on people who like iPhones, or Millennials who use social media religiously, but...

There's an immediate gratification element to using a social app, or buying a toy. Well, immediately after a 12 hour wait for the latter, but still...you don't get that with voting. That's more of an investment activity.

Yeah, and I think part of it is that a lot of Millennials still don't have the usual roster of adult obligations like paying back student loans or putting away money for retirement. Investing, like you said. A lot of the younger Millennials probably don't vote because they don't fully realize how they're being screwed over on things like student loan interest rates or the talks about privatizing Medicare. The issues don't affect them immediately.

I want to get your take on two possible election outcomes. If the Democrats manage to continue their winning streak with a Clinton victory, what do you see your political involvement looking like after November?

After, like, a large celebration? [laughs] I don't know. I would obviously breathe a huge sigh of relief, but...um...God, I don't know. I haven't really thought about it. And maybe that's bad. Maybe my reaction would be, "Disaster averted! Nothing to do here." Which is not true.

Now, if Trump wins, how does that inform what you'll do?

If Trump wins, I think I'm gonna move out of the country. [laughs]

You wouldn't be fleeing alone.

Yeah. I mean, most people are probably laughing about it, but for me personally, as a gay man of color, in an interracial gay relationship...I'm lucky I live in one of the most liberal cities in the United States, but there's only so many protections that the city and state can provide. You know? I have no idea what this country's gonna be like under a Trump presidency. It would probably cause me psychological damage to stay here for four years.

If it weren't for Trump and you felt like you had the luxury of focusing more closely on the issues at the heart of the Democratic side, what issues would you want to see more meaningfully addressed?

There are so many. One big one is institutionalized racism and police brutality. Everything the Black Lives Matter movement has been spotlighting. The attacks on Planned Parenthood. Upholding a woman's right to choose. The economic inequality that Bernie touched on and the giant corporate welfare program that we have right now, that a lot of people don't even realize exists. I'm hoping that people like Bernie Sanders and Elizabeth Warren can keep Hillary Clinton honest and on-point with all of these things. I don't think those two have enough allies within Congress who are like them, but...

That could change if Millennials start running for local offices in the coming years. Sure, there's that likelihood of young people becoming less idealistic as they get older, but if these issues persist and don't improve...I don't know. Maybe that could be a catalyst for a new wave of leftward political energy. Do you think Millennials may retain some of their idealism after dealing with hardship?

Probably not. I think this process repeats itself every four years. Right before election time, people get fired up about the issues and then they

go away when it's all over. Unfortunately.
Involvement peaks right before an election. I wish
there was some way of changing that.

.

GINA

26 years old
Restaurant Manager
Baltimore, Maryland

July 2, 2016

INTERIOR. A small coffee shop. Shelves. Board games. A new espresso machine. The place hasn't opened to the public yet, but it will in six days.

Tell me a little bit about where your hometown.

[laughs] Okay, if you're sure.

Oh yeah. Lay it on me.

So, I was born in Baltimore, what I think of fondly as white trash Baltimore. Where a lot of neighbors' parents were on hard drugs. But they still had cute houses with yards. So, it was kind of a strange area. And my parents moved us out of Baltimore when I was 10, and we went to a town that, I shit you not, is called "Factoryville, Pennsylvania." It's in the woods. Population: 1,013, last I checked.[1]

All the adults there are Republicans. Even some of the teachers were Republicans, at my high school. Literally, they're right there, in the teacher's union, voting Republican. One of them was interviewed by The Daily Show, back during the Obama/McCain election, because she went to a Sarah Palin rally and said something really ignorant about how Obama was gonna "get into office and put on his turban and we're all gonna be shocked." Now, she said "shocked" but people thought she said "shot," so it was all over political TV. *She* was all over TV, for a good week, and I

---

[1] In 2010, the population of Factoryville, PA was 1,158 people.

was, like, "That is an English teacher from my high school." She was the advisor of the newspaper when I was the editor.

Do you have a grasp of how many Democrats there were in Factoryville, at the time when you were growing up there?

We were a lonely bunch. I mean, our town went red every time. My mom is a liberal democrat and my dad...uh...my dad is obsessed with Donald Trump. [pause] They're not married anymore. [laughs] But, like, my dad is an immigrant named Julio who goes to Trump rallies. So...that's a thing. That really happens. I'm like, "Dad, Trump wouldn't *like* you. Trump would expect you to make him a taco."

So, anyway, I grew up thinking that my dad was an idiot, and my mom was brilliant, and that I should definitely vote Democrat, and not just because she told me too. My mom, the nice parent, was a Democrat, so I figured I must be a Democrat too. So I was a little kid, being like, "Go Clinton!" I was *really* into it.

So, being part of the Democratic minority in Factoryville, how inspired did you feel when it came to getting involved in the political process? Starting as early as high school, how did you feel about political involvement?

I was pretty fired up. My first election that I voted

in was the Obama/McCain race, like a lot of us. But when I was in Factoryville, I was the editor of the high school newspaper, and I would usually get to write whatever I wanted, and while I usually didn't go into politics, I decided to try putting out a feminist column. And this got me bullied a lot. Like, to the point where teachers would bully me. I had one teacher verbally rip my article up, in front of the entire class, until I cried. Just because he didn't like that I was writing about feminism. And, I mean, it wasn't even a good article! It was just a dumb fluff piece.

And yet, your teacher went out of their way to trash the whole thing and humiliate you because-

He thought it was inappropriate for me to stereotype men and lump them together. And I was just thinking, "Wow. You're really making a big difference in the way I perceive men right now, you piece of shit." Like, I still haven't forgiven that man. He was in his forties and he bullied a ninth grader.

So, like, that's where I grew up. Where girls who asked questions were bullied. That's how I got *really* militant. [laughs] And I had one teacher who was really into that. He was like, "You should do that. You should stay militant. Let me fuel this fire." And right after 9/11, when we were about to start bombing Afghanistan, I wrote this long essay about how Bush was doing the wrong thing, and that teacher made me mail it to the White House.

Actually, it was with this same teacher that I really had my first "glimpse" at politics. Around the time I was in his class, Bush was campaigning on behalf of our awful local congressman. Bush actually came to Factoryville to host a campaign fundraiser for the guy, and my teacher took us to see him. And we waited, and waited, and waited, figuring the president was probably gonna come out and say hello. But he never did. He waved from the back of a car when the motorcade drove by, and that was it, after we'd waited for almost five hours. But it was still kind of neat to see all that ceremony.

Right next to me, where we were all waiting, there was a reporter from the local paper, and I started talking with him about the whole thing, and I was actually quoted, in our town paper, just *shit talking* our Republican congressman. And this guy, he was a powerful figure. Like, he determined who got home repair subsidies after the town got flooded, and a lot of the time, it was how you voted that sealed your deal. He was a corrupt son of a bitch. And I said all kinds of bad things about him. It was a big bold quote on the side of the article. But that's how I found out who the other local Democrats were. They came up to me and were, like, "You rock." All three of them. And I was, like, "Cool! Thank you! We're all gonna be lynched!"

Did this create any problems for your family? Were your folks worried about you?

Oh, well, my parents moved to Florida after I graduated from high school. No connection, I'm sure. [laughs] But no, it actually turned out alright, because the following year, my name was cleared when our congressman, the one I shit talked, he got convicted in this big scandal. Trying to strangle his prostitute mistress to death in DC. This was after a year of campaigning on family values. Of course.

So, once you escaped Factoryville, how did it feel to be participating in your first real election in a new and less familiar place?

It was perplexing, but in a good way. I moved up here, and suddenly, it's, "Oh, I'm now surrounded by like-minded people? This is strange." I was almost *less* engaged that way. But then I experienced political arguing on Facebook for the first time, and that drew me right back in. Over half the population of Factoryville is on my Friends list, so...

How do you go about that? It's something that a lot of people, particularly Millennials, have to deal with. Talking politics and disagreeing with each other on social media.

At this point, I've posted enough militant feminist stuff that most of Factoryville has unfollowed me without unfriending me. The people who see it are the people who want to see it. I have one friend from Baltimore, Tommy, he turned out to be the most privileged lawyer, he's such a twat...but I love him. We'll flip out at each other on Facebook, and then it's, like, "Nice talking with you, bro." When his dad had heart surgery, I was, like, "Tommy, are you okay?" and he goes, "Thanks, ya commie."

How do you feel about the tone and discussion around the 2016 election thus far?

Well, one thing I've been surprised by this year is, in spite of all the horrible negativity, I feel like there's been more of a discussion about voting actually works.

As in, understanding how much certain votes "count" in the various stages of the election?

Exactly. How some votes do count and could absolutely tip the scales. That wasn't something people seemed to be talking about as much during 2008 and 2012. Back then, I didn't even know what a superdelegate was. And today, we're debating whether or not superdelegates should still be a thing. We're tossing around words like "oligarchy." We are in an oligarchy right now, so it makes sense that we're talking more seriously about whether one person's vote absolutely counts. I mean, I believe it does, obviously, but it's a sign of the times. At the very least, it signals that most people *want* their votes to count. And that's a healthy sign for democracy. But at the same time, that just makes the process itself...the caucuses, the open primaries, closed primaries, superdelegate system...it makes the whole thing feel so disheartening and hopelessly messy.

Why do you think political mechanics are suddenly at the forefront of our attention? It really does feel like this election cycle has been all about better understanding the nitty-gritty details of how our process works.

I don't think we talked about the process as much back then because I don't think there was a "bad guy." You know? I wouldn't have been heartbroken if McCain had won. In fact, I was almost conflicted, until he picked Sarah Palin and then he—*they*—had to be stopped. Because she was the goddamn devil: minus a few IQ points, because she couldn't run Hell. But until that point, the election just felt like seeing what the American people wanted. This time, there is literally a bad guy. A guy who hates more than half the country! Like, if you take all the women, all the Hispanics, all the black people...that's a humongous percentage of the electorate.

That's an interesting theory because you'd think, given the urgency of this election, a lot of people who ideologically oppose Trump would want to table the conversation about the electoral process reform until after the "bad guy" was soundly defeated. But instead, we're seeing this wave of political despondency frothing up during the final months of the election months, and it's freaking out Democratic leaders who are anxious about voter turnout in November. I mean, you said it yourself: the electoral process is a disheartening mess.

It absolutely is, and this whole national conversation about how the process works hasn't made me feel better or more empowered. It leaves me feeling even more confused. I feel like we don't actually pick who becomes president. The parties do. The party officials have a lot more to do with deciding who gets to run for president than we, the people, do. Even the Electoral College is outdated in an Internet age. I mean, with the Internet, a direct election[2] is actually possible. And yet, we're farther from it than ever with this superdelegate system determining the primary outcome. It's bullshit. Superdelegates are bullshit. They can swing an election. That's inappropriate. But the reason they're in place is to prevent a grassroots movement from taking hold, which literally takes the last remaining peaceful revolutionary power out of the average citizen's hands.

One thing Susan Sarandon said this year—sometimes she's just fucking crazy, but often she says some really good stuff—she said she wasn't too worried because if Trump wins, the revolution starts immediately. And I thought, "Well, historically speaking, our country is overdue for a revolution." But I also believed that as a democratic nation, we didn't need one because democracy facilitates a peaceful transition of

---

[2] In a direct election, there are no representatives who vote on behalf of the common voters. Citizens vote for themselves, directly, for the candidates whom they support.

power.

I say this with a grain of salt, but...the Democrats, as a party, are supposed to be the good guys. And yet, they cling to this superdelegate system to prevent "street" Democrats from making any real decisions. That's not good guy behavior. And so, part of me wants to vote third party, since Maryland isn't a swing state. The whole thing is just a big fucking mess.

To play devil's advocate, on behalf of some other anti-Trump people I've spoken to, one could argue that if the Republicans had a superdelegate system in place, they could have prevented Trump—the "bad guy" of the 2016 election—from grabbing the nomination.

Which could prevent the apocalypse, sure. But honestly, if Trump is who the majority of Republican voters want to run...that's who the party should run. That is how a democracy works.

All of the frustrations you've expressed are reflective of what I've been hearing from many of the other Millennials whom I've spoken with.

I hope we don't have to revolt. But...we're a country that was raised on Les Miz[3] at this age. We know what we're up against. You know. We can wave a flag back and forth like the best of 'em.

---

[3] "Les Miz" is shorthand for the Victor Hugo musical *Les Misérables*, an epic of proletariat tribulations during the French Revolution. Nothing ominous about a reference like that.

[laughs] I feel like, if something doesn't happen...I don't imagine some kind of uprising going down because Americans are so fucking comfortable. If we were a little poorer, a little less well-fed, a little less entertained, a little less caffeinated and Netflixed—I'm part of the problem—then we might better see how much political power has been taken from us over the past 50 years.

But in spite of that relinquishment of power and this sad state of affairs you describe, you're still committed to voting in this election?

Yes, and in every subsequent election.

How do you feel about voting in this election?

It is my duty. Not my civic duty, but my duty to the country that I wish I had. And if I hear from any of my friends that they're not voting, I will tear them a new one. "You don't vote, then you don't say fucking shit." That's how I feel about not voting. "You didn't do your job? Then shut the fuck up." My face is getting red right now. Talking about politics makes me want to throw things. I'm Spanish, I'm hot-blooded. I mean, you've heard me raise my voice when we *agree* on things.

I really would love to read some of these other interviews you've done and find that perhaps Hillary isn't the only way to defeat Trump. That young people can vote for whoever they want and Trump would still lose. But I've really gotten to a place where I think, if you're not voting for Hillary, you're basically voting for Trump. Unless you're in Maryland. We're not a swing state, we're gonna vote for Hillary, it's gonna be fine. But then, if everybody thinks like that...I have so many friends who are adamant about voting third party because we're not a swing state, then I'm like, "If you're the one person who tips our state vote to Trump..." That's my concern. If we go independent, we *become* a swing state. And now that Bernie has lost, I think it's okay that those of us who supported him can come to a place and concede that he didn't win. I liked him best, I really did. But the people didn't elect him. I believe in a system where the person who gets the most votes wins, like 'em or not. I cried when Bush won the second time! Wept like a baby.

But now...I'm excited about Hillary. Even though Bernie shared more of my values, even though Hillary's not nearly as liberal as I am, I think, since she saw how close Bernie came to stealing her thunder, she's manipulative enough to adopt some of his positions, and that's great. Be a sponge, Hil. She's not evil. More like, "Oh! The people are more liberal than I thought. Maybe, to capture the votes that Bernie soaked up, I need to be more progressive on trans people. I need to stop wearing $12,000 jackets to poverty dinners." I think she's going to find her way further left. In fact, I think a further left Hillary is even better than Bernie.

A lot of the people I've talked to, part of their frustration with the system is how a lot of politicians will say anything to get elected and then once they get into office, their campaign promises are broken and their conduct reflects the values of the wealthy people who funded their campaigns. If President Hillary Clinton were to do this, to revert back to a centrist position after being sworn in, how would that affect your political involvement?

Well, here's the thing. I don't think she has as much freedom to do that as other presidents have. Look at the things we harangue Hillary for. Like her jacket. I just picked her apart for that! We don't pick apart male presidents over the suits they wear. Ever since the primary started, we haven't heard nearly as much commentary about Trump's appearance. I mean, the guy looks like an Oompa-Loompa with bad hair. He actually repulses me. I see him, and I think that I will never want to have sex again. The idea that someone has seen Donald Trump naked makes me want to kill myself. And then he said that thing about wanting to fuck his own daughter?[4] The man is repugnant! But because he is a man, none of this stuff gains traction. People don't focus on it for more than a few minutes. Meanwhile, Hillary wears a very tasteful albeit overpriced jacket, and it's a trending topic on Twitter and Facebook. "Hillary wore an expensive jacket to a Harlem fundraiser." Yeah! Hillary's one of the richest white ladies in the

---

[4] Indeed, during a 2006 appearance on *The View*, Donald Trump said that if Ivanka Trump weren't his daughter, he would likely be dating her. Especially if Playboy featured her on a magazine cover. It was an uncomfortable moment.

country. Duh, she has expensive clothes! What was she *saying* at the fundraiser? Was it ignorant? Maybe. But she's trying! So, I really think, if she says certain things in her campaign, she's not going to have the liberty to do whatever she wants as president. She's gonna have to stick to that shit, or she will be a one-term president. And that's hopeful. It's kind of evil, too, the double standard. But it could force her to "get things done" in a meaningful and progressive way.

In future elections, hopefully—if we continue educating ourselves about the mechanics of the political process, how it works, how it became this way—hopefully the process will change for the better. Maybe the next wave of women in politics will be judged just as scrupulously or generously as their male counterparts. What other changes would you like to see, in how our elections work?

I would like to be able to see the literal number of humans who voted for this person and that person in future primaries and elections. In every state. That alone should determine who the delegates get behind. I mean, that's how most of us thought the electoral process worked, but of course, that's not how it works. That's a very simple thing to want.

DAVE

28 years old
National Guardsman
Derry, New Hampshire

May 27, 2016

INTERIOR. A dining room with family pictures on the walls. The neighborhood is wooded, quiet. Leaves are falling. A dog barks somewhere distant.

When we talked on the phone, you mentioned that you and your folks moved to Derry quite a few years back. What brought you here? Tell me about your childhood.

You're pretty much looking at it. I grew up in this general area. I was born over in Lawrence, Massachusetts, which...I don't know if you know anything about this area, but Lawrence is a shithole. I like to tell people that the reason we moved out of Lawrence is, my parents...there was a scenario where they thought I was almost abducted. This guy was driving around, staring at me while I was sitting out on the front steps. So, we ended up moving across state lines to the bottom of New Hampshire. I grew up here. Went to college in one of the neighboring towns, and then, moved back. Haven't been able to get out. Because I don't have any money. So, yeah.

Apart from time in the military and some time in Ireland, I've been in this area my entire life.

What was the political climate around here like, when you were growing up?

My dad likes to claim he's an Independent, but he's pretty much a Republican. My mom...I don't really talk to her much about it. I feel like local political involvement is something you get in smaller towns. Smaller than towns like Derry, or Lawrence. Like, when you hear about the mayor of Lawrence selling police cruisers to other precincts all around the country, just to make a profit,[1] and then getting indicted for it...people around here don't really participate in politics much. They know what's going on, but they seem more interested in bitching about it than really doing anything personally.

When you turned 18 and became eligible to vote, did politics seem like something you could tangibly take part in?

Yeah. I was very politically interested in high school. I took an AP U.S. Government class and we did weekly debates on all the hot-button issues.

What interested you about politics at that age?

I was young and naive. [laughs] I was thinking, "*Oh, I have an opinion and people might actually listen to me...at this age.*" It was fun to be active and talk about those opinions with other people. And I sort of liked the back-and-forth, and the ability to have a dialogue with somebody else. But as I've gotten older, it's been...I've enjoyed it less and less, and I find it more of a hassle now, and I'm usually not willing to mention anything because most people

---

[1] This was actually done by the Lawrence Police Department, which illegally traded 13 city vehicles for four Chevy Impalas. However, the used car salesman that brokered the swap was an associate of former Lawrence Mayor William "Willie" Lantigua.

get so vitriolic about everything. I mean, I've had numerous Facebook fights with my military recruiter because he just immediately resorts to ad hominem attacks. Like, "You're an idiot!" and I'm like, "Where did this come from? What have I done? Because I have a different belief than you, I'm a moron?"

Do you remember a single moment in which you felt a little older and less naive?

When I joined the military. It wasn't even the government itself so much as the way the military acted. By the time I got out, my takeaway was, "Most people in general are looking out for themselves, but if this applies to the people leading the military as well, that's even worse because they're just using men and women for their own ends." I had no idea what to do anymore.

And then there was the financial crash in 2008. At the time, I didn't really understand the scope of the whole thing, but as the smoke cleared, I'm like, "We sent Wall Street hundreds of billions of dollars in the form of a bailout...I'm $60,000 in debt for a degree that's done nothing for me, and yet, I'm somehow complaining because I'm getting the short end of the stick?" You know?

I had a conversation with my dad the other day. In 1969, he was 12 years old, working a part-time job, making something like $3.15 an hour. And I did the math, went online to look at the inflation.

Want to know how much that is nowadays?

How much?

$20 an hour. At 12 years, he was making money worth $20 in buying power. And today, I'm a veteran with a master's degree and I'm lucky if I can find a job that pays $16 an hour. I have a five-year degree—the military paid for two years of it—and I'm still that deep in debt. And when I bring this stuff up, a lot of people are like, "All generations had it rough. You don't know what you're talking about." And I'm like, "No. Look at the wage stagnation. Look at the price of housing. Look at the cost of education. It's getting worse."

Why do you think this "things could be worse" race-to-the-bottom mentality has proven so hard to shake? Why are people resistant to concede that we're in a rut right now?

Well, it's more of a confirmation bias. Each generation wants to say it's had a rougher time than any others, and I'm...it's not the Greatest Generation with all the World War II vets. They can never be rewarded enough, for all the things they went through as a generation. It's more the Baby Boomers and even the Generation X'ers that are looking at us and saying, "Oh, you guys have it easy compared to us." And I just want to go, "...*in what way?* Apart from the fact that you had the ability to establish yourselves as members of society, as adults capable of providing for yourselves. That your parents gave you social security and Medicare."

So I think it's just...I hate using this term, but it's privilege. People use that word for so many things today, but with the Boomers, I think they're blinded by their privilege.

Which is an ironic accusation, because our generation tends to be thought of as recipients of undeserved privilege. Like, our parents broke their backs for us, and now we've developed into these entitled little shits.

I've been called a socialist because I want to vote for Bernie Sanders. And I'm a registered Republican. [laughs]

I want to dig a little deeper into the way that you and I are perceived broadly, as Millennials. What do you think most Boomers and Generation X'ers misunderstand about our generation?

Easy. Our want for free education and health care doesn't mean that we actually think those things are free. I think most of us realize that even if those things happen, we're not gonna reap many benefits, if any. There's probably not gonna be an answer for our generation, but I think there could be an answer for our kids. A lot of us are at that point where we're thinking of settling down and having kids. But, it's like...the polls just seem to say that we want free stuff.

What the older generation doesn't understand is, we're *already* paying for that stuff, and we want to pay for it in a more graduated way. It's $60,000 out of your pocket for school, right now, versus $60,000 in taxes, over the next 40 odd years. This perception of Millennial entitlement, I think it's the older generation feeding that. And, I hate to say this, but I think we'll be better off when they're gone. Because, as far as progressive issues go, whether it's equal rights or the tax stuff...we won't have to deal with them trying to put a stop to something that'll actually benefit the greater good.

It does seem like there are two mainstream outlooks on paving the road for our kids and their kids. The first is, like, "I want your life to be easier than mine has been," and the second goes, "Screw you. I suffered and so should you." How do you advocate for helping the coming generations when you're talking to people whose outlook on other generations is basically, "fuck 'em?"

Well, it's tough when you're talking to people who are mostly gonna be dead in 30 years and won't be around to watch all the fallout from these bad decisions and indecisions happening right now. It's...I...unless you have some sort of magnetic leader like Martin Luther King...it's time. We're still fighting racism, decades after the civil rights movement. You have to wait for the right outlook to spread. Look at gay marriage. It was only legalized in Massachusetts within the last five years. And it just goes to show that no matter how long and hard you've been fighting for a cause, the most you can hope for is that the minds you're trying to change will absorb all the information you're putting out there, about the cause, and change faster. My parents' generation mostly looks at Muslims as bad people, and chances are, no matter how many statistics you throw at them, most of their generation is still gonna feel the same way in a few years.

So you feel that the Boomers are holding us back. Though you're in the tank for Bernie, who's something of an outlier when it comes to...actually, I'm not even sure if Bernie is young enough to qualify as a Baby Boomer. Either way, as a candidate, does he represent a big step forward for ushering in the changes you want to see? Could he speed up the clock, so to speak?

I think so. And, just to be clear, I'm not one of the Bernie Bros who think he can do no wrong, or that everything he wants to do will be easy and work out properly. I know that at some point, I'm going to end up paying more in taxes. I'm willing to do that if it means my kids won't be in as much debt as I've been. In fact, I'd be willing to donate my paycheck and live on the street if it meant that all of the banking executives behind the 2008 crash would go to prison. Because if you, me, or any of us did something stupid like pushing those bubble loans, or combining the crappy stocks into...what's the word?

The CDOs?[2] We'd be in jail indefinitely. Unless you're Jamie Dimon's nephew and you haven't told me. Then I'd be the only one in jail.

Exactly. And I'd love to see Hillary Clinton indicted for the email server thing. I mean...Edward Snowden is considered a traitor and living in Russia because the government says he maliciously leaked classified information. I'm all for freedom of information, and it really seems like he believed that those leaks would make us a better and more informed people. A healthier country. But Clinton, she jeopardizes classified information out of stupidity, then lies about it for the entire primary cycle, and she gets a free pass. How does that make sense? Obviously, the way the Republicans are going on about the issue, they're just trying to take Clinton down for their own gain. But as a legal precedent, seeing Clinton get indicted...I mean, Enron was already bankrupt when we went after them. What happens to these people? Crime at a corporate or state level ruins more people's lives than one drug dealer ever could.

This makes me think of the political polarity you mentioned earlier. We become so convinced that everything the other side says is wrong and moronic that

---

[2] CDO is an acronym for "Collateralized Debt Obligation." This is essentially a sack of shitty mortgages, bonds, and loans. The CDO was instrumental in fueling the 2008 housing market implosion. Banks and ratings agencies were complicit in mislabeling CDOs and selling them to unsuspecting investors.

even when someone on your own side does something
that warrants criticism, people attack you for voicing
those criticisms. The circular firing squad. And you're
like, "Wait a second. We're on the same team!"

Right. And Clinton's being investigated by two
Obama appointees, so, this isn't just the usual GOP
anti-Clinton propaganda. She's being investigated
by a Democratic administration, for something
that...if you or I did it, we'd be put in prison for the
rest of our lives, if not executed for treason.

Snowden did make that point.[3] If we did this, we'd be
lucky to get a jail sentence. And I feel like that truth
illustrates the dynamic that's riling up the country.
People who belong to this elite echelon, whether it's
politics, finance, tech...there's this implicit
understanding that they live in a different universe with
different rules, standards of living, protections than the
rest of us enjoy. I've heard other people our age express
this. It may explain why some of those Millennials are
less committed to things like voting in elections. Because
they feel it's meaningless. That our leaders will just do
what they want, regardless of what we demand. But
you're not discouraged enough to totally drop out of the
political process. How do you feel about the insinuation
that the process is hopeless and your vote doesn't matter?

Oh, just because I'm participating, doesn't mean
that I *don't* feel that way. I vote because, I mean, I

---

[3] "Break classification rules for the public's benefit, and you
could be exiled. Do it for personal benefit, and you could be
President." Edward Snowden. June 1, 2016.

214

don't have enough time to volunteer. I'm barely making enough money to cover my bills. But things are close enough in the race right now that I feel like my vote...if I could be one of the 48% that voted for Sanders, as opposed to the 50% that voted for Hillary...at least I could be part of the number that's saying, "We don't believe in everything the Clinton Democrats have been selling."

So, if Bernie manages to win the nomination and he gets elected-

I think things are gonna change less than people think they will, if Bernie gets elected, which is a long shot, yeah. But I also think there's a greater chance that certain things will improve, radically. If not during his presidency, than in the near future. But if Hillary gets elected, we're gonna have a Democratic Bush administration, with stupid mistakes getting made and lots of scandals within the administration. And if Trump gets elected...it's not even Trump that worries me. It's his supporters. I feel like half of the country is gonna turn into a literal lynch mob. Because I don't think Trump is spouting all this crap maliciously. I think he's just an idiot, surrounded by too many yes-men telling him to keep going.

Yes-men. That also reminds me of what you cited earlier, about politics becoming more black and white. Fewer concessions to the other side. It makes sense, if you're surrounded by enablers, you'll seldom apologize or admit to error.

And you can never get a straight answer! I'll bet a lot of people would immediately vote for someone who was able to say that they were wrong about something. Say what you will about Paul Ryan, but he went on national television and admitted that he was wrong about his opinions on gay marriage, poverty, stuff like that. And who knows if it was genuine or calculated, but to appear in a public forum and say that he was wrong about major platform issues carried a huge perceived risk. Imagine if Bernie Sanders publicly admitted that he wasn't tough enough during the Veterans Affairs medical coverage fight.[4] He was part of the committee to fix the VA and I would argue that he had too much faith in the system correcting itself to ensure that people were actually covered. But I think if he came right out today and said, "I wasn't tough enough on the VA issues and that's not gonna happen again," he'd get even more support from veterans than he already has.

That's all that people want: a little accountability. We've got it in our jobs, we can be fired for not making quotas or whatever. I don't think it's asking too much to hold politicians to similar standards.

---

[4] The 2014 VA scandal, in which dozens of veterans died while waiting for care at the Phoenix VA health facility, happened under Bernie Sanders' watch. He was chairman of the Senate Veterans Affairs Committee at the time, and, by his own admission, Sanders had tremendous faith in the government's ability to step in and rectify the situation.

But with the 96% re-election rate for incumbents, good luck.

Where do you think this resistance to accountability comes from? You've just outlined some very compelling reasons to rethink the idea that holding oneself accountable is political suicide.

Because the people who won't admit that they're wrong—even when they are wrong—they're too afraid that the result won't go their way. That it'll help the other candidate. And at a time like this, with so many people fed up with phony politicians who lie or even refuse to listen to people...I *don't* think holding oneself accountable will automatically boost the other candidate's numbers. Hillary admitting she was wrong about the emails would be good for her. She's looked at as untrustworthy, but coming clean like that could help her change that perception.

She could use a boost. The support numbers for both Clinton and Trump—among Millennials—are not encouraging. Even though Clinton is the relative favorite, there appears to be an enthusiasm gap between now and 2008, when Obama energized young voters. I wonder if that's partially on account of Clinton's platform, and partially because our generation now outnumbers Boomers but has lacks a presence in elected office. It's rare to see a 30-something Senator. As Millennials grow older, do you see their participation in politics changing? There's a lot for Millennials to be upset about and fired up about. Some people will inevitably ride those waves of frustration into positions of power.

A constitutional amendment would help. You have to be at least 30 to get into the Senate, but you've got 18 year olds running for mayor. Whether or not they're ready for that is another discussion entirely, but at least they're running. Some of them have even won, and done well. But it's very hard to run as a young candidate and win over older voters because most of them will probably say, "This kid doesn't have enough life experience to govern. I have more experience." Regardless of what "experience" even means in that case. And I mean, four to six years of college...it might seem like your kid is partying all the time, but I bet your kid has absorbed just as much information—from different sources—as you did when you were smoking weed in your parents' basement and waiting for the new Pink Floyd album.

So what do you think "experience" means in politics today?

I'm not sure, because you can have many years of experience in foreign policy, but what does that mean? Accomplishments? How many fewer times you fucked up compared to the previous person? "When I was working for the State Department, I only got this many people killed, unlike my predecessor, who got *this* many people killed." Too much experience in one area can be a bad thing, because you can be unwilling to listen to other people's advice and too set in your own beliefs. I think one of the Roosevelts said, "I like to surround myself with people much smarter than I am." It goes to show you that even previously, the whole yes-men issue we talked about earlier was something that had to be actively fought. Experience is overrated if you don't have the knowledge, the common sense, or the help to make smart decisions going forward.

Thinking about voting in this coming election, it's empirically clear that more Millennials need to participate in the electoral process to precipitate any of the changes you've mentioned, including something like a constitutional amendment on the minimum age for a Senator. When you meet Millennials who say they're not voting, what's your reaction?

"Why?" Before I judge them, I like to know their reasoning. I'm probably not gonna change anyone's mind. Most people only listen to other opinions so they can fight back with an argument and defend how they feel. But I still want to know why they're not voting.

The most common thing I hear is that people feel like their votes don't matter. And with this election...can you blame them? The way the primary race is set up, people's votes aren't equal. If your state has a closed primary, Independents can't vote. Living in a regular state or a swing state determines how much your vote counts for. If you're one of the last states to vote, you might not even get to vote at all if a winner has already emerged and the other candidates give up. And regardless of how you feel about the superdelegates, the fact that hundreds of people pledged to support Hillary Clinton before any votes were ever counted and the media blew up those numbers...it left a lot of people thinking their support for Bernie was a waste of time. That getting involved was a waste of time. I don't blame people for feeling fed up and hopeless about voting. If they're just lazy, that's another thing, but there's a lot to be depressed about, the way our elections are run.

That depression and hopelessness could lead to an exodus from both parties after this election. But at the moment, it feels to me like publicly revealing yourself as an Independent, a Man Without Party, can earn you a lot of harsh words from folks who strongly identify as loyal Democrats and Republicans.

I mean, yeah, there are some differences between the two big parties, but most leaders from those parties are too corrupt and full of shit to be leading the country. And I think that's really what it comes down to. No hesitation. I'm not a conspiracy theorist, but by forcing people into these narrow party lines, that's how leaders control you. And it's how they keep viable third party candidates from rising up.

What do you think it will take for a third party candidate to become a true electoral contender?

As much as this could be a doomsday scenario in this election, if Clinton gets indicted and Trump wins and screws everything up...there would be a *massive* exodus from both parties. If Clinton wins the nomination and becomes president, I think it would take several more election cycles, but if the other parties keep putting up alternative candidates and the pool of jaded and disappointed Independents keeps growing...it's gonna happen eventually. The more people feel like there's no good party line to toe, the more acceptable it'll feel to go somewhere else. I think too many people invest their identity into being a Democrat or a Republican. I forgot to change my registration in time for the primary, but after this election, I will be an Independent.

Do you think the growth of another party—any party— would be a true turning point for us?

I hope so. I think it would change the way we discuss these issues with each other. And that's the thing. We really need to figure out how to talk with each other again.

"The cradle rocks above an abyss and common sense tells us that our existence is but a brief crack of light between two eternities of darkness. Although the two are identical twins, man, as a rule, views the prenatal abyss with more calm than the one he is heading for...

I know, however, of a young chronophobiac who experienced something like panic when looking for the first time at homemade movies that had been taken a few weeks before his birth. He saw a world that was practically unchanged – the same house, the same people – and then realized that he did not exist there at all and that nobody mourned his absence.

He caught a glimpse of his mother waving from an upstairs window, and that unfamiliar gesture disturbed him, as if it were some mysterious farewell."

Vladimir Nabokov
Speak, Memory, 1966

CONCLUSIONS

So, more than 200 pages later, what *do* Millennials care about?

There are two ways to approach the question. You can focus on the hard political issues that Millennials harbor strong feelings about. Or you can consider this question something closer to a spiritual inquiry.

Here, I'll apply both approaches in concluding what my interviews revealed, and what those conclusions foreshadow.

ONE CLEAN WORLD

The issue that came up in most of my Millennial interviews wasn't student loan debt or unemployment. It was climate change.

I was surprised by how many of the young people whom I spoke with expressed concern about global warming and its devastating effects on our environment. But I shouldn't have found this surprising. Primal self-interest is a stronger force of governance than many of us will admit, and Millennials have a unique reason to worry about climate change. The ravages of unmitigated climate change—floods, heat waves, food shortages, and rampant disease—are projected to occur within the average Millennial's lifetime. Some of the young adults featured in this book had personally experienced the force of climate change before I met them. Martin and his family lost their home and most of their possessions to a hurricane that gestated in the warming waters of the Gulf of Mexico and became a monster storm. Jesse and Dani are both settled in states that have experienced severe drought conditions and water crises in recent years. The town of Denton, Texas, where I spent a day interviewing Stephanie and another day walking around, has become a battleground for anti-fracking activists hell bent on preventing energy companies from drilling for natural gas in the Denton area.[1] So for Millennials, doing everything possible to counteract the effects of climate change isn't some idealistic ambition—it's the pragmatic thing to do.

Less clear was how Millennials felt about the pragmatism of showing up and voting for candidates who promised to make climate change action a top priority. While I didn't encounter

---

[1] In May of 2015, lightning struck a natural gas well in Denton and created a monstrous blaze that threatened to engulf the homes of many residents. Several of those residents had no idea that there was a gas well so close to their neighborhood. Incidents like this put the growth of the local anti-fracking movement in perspective.

many self-described non-voters, what I did hear most often, upon bringing up voting, was alienation. Many of the Millennials I spoke with claimed that they didn't feel represented across the political spectrum. Granted, "spectrum" may be the wrong word here, considering how white our government still is.[2] But this feeling of marginalization among Millennials seemed to reach beyond race, gender, age, and even ideology. The electoral process itself has left Millennials in a state of frustration and apprehension. Lee, Owen, and Wesley cited the issue of campaign finance regulations, or rather, the lack thereof. Others lamented the heavy-handed role that party officials can play when it's time to pick candidates for national elections. Look no further than the inherently undemocratic superdelegate system still used by the Democrats, which is designed to prevent a grassroots insurgency from upsetting the party rank during an election year.[3] As Gina said during our conversation, that system strips voters of an essential power—the power to revolt against the status quo, nonviolently.

If both major political parties now rely on wealthy benefactors to bankroll their candidates' campaigns—an arrangement that carries an

---

[2] The Pew Research Center puts the 114th U.S. Congress at 83% white. And here's the kicker—this is the most diverse Congress in U.S. history!

[3] Former Democratic National Committee Chair Debbie Wasserman Schultz admitted this during the 2016 Democratic presidential primary race.

implicit *quid pro quo* provision—or if one party keeps superdelegates around to uphold the agenda of the party officials, voters be damned, then one has to ask, why *should* the average Millennial have faith in the efficacy of voting?

This is where it's necessary to jump from the hard issues to the spiritual values expressed by the Millennials I spoke with.

In spite of their anxieties and the disparity of their formative experiences, the Millennials I interviewed wanted to make their world a better place. That might sound like the sort of mission statement that tech companies have now appropriated to sell inbound marketing software and automated burrito deliveries, but there's a big difference. CEOs like Marc Benioff and John Zimmer will often wax poetic about making *the* world a better place, but the Millennials featured in this book were more concerned with improving *their* worlds. It's easy to forget that altruism doesn't have to come in the form of grand and sweeping change. It can—and should—be localized too. Look at Jose's dream of opening a gym and teaching martial arts to neighborhood kids. Imagine Kevin and Olivia fostering friendships between campus faith groups and others in the UMASS Amherst area. Or better yet, consider something that Landon said to me on that figuratively *and* literally shitty Greyhound bus ride from Las Vegas to Salt Lake City, when I asked what he and Katie hoped to find and hold onto in their new home. "Jobs that don't turn us into assholes."

Therein lies the brightest glimmer of hope that I believe this years-long endeavor has yielded. For all the distressing events that have rattled the Earth for Millennials—economic recession, natural disasters, terrorist attacks, perpetual war, the corrupting influence of big money in politics—the Millennial generation doesn't strike me as a sad bastard generation. The Millennials whom I spoke with were feeling ground down and weary, but they weren't giving up on idealism. Dave, the National Guardsmen from Derry, New Hampshire embodied this better than anyone, which is why I decided to close the book with his interview. The guy could have chosen to be consumed by bitterness, but Dave's disdain for arrogant Baby Boomers and the lack of accountability in Washington DC and elite society was counterbalanced by an expressed desire to ensure some measure of stability for the next generation of American—to spare them the pains and indignities that have shaped the average Millennial's coming-of-age experience.

GETTING REAL, GOING BIG

Now that we know a little more about the Millennial generation, the challenge to political officials and parties is clear. How does one earn the trust and enthusiasm of Millennial voters like Dave or any of the others profiled in this book?

The Millennials are often described as Democratic Party loyalists. This is fallacy. The majority of Millennial voters have only had the chance to cast ballots in one or two presidential elections, and one round of midterm races. That's not enough polling data from which to draw rock solid conclusions about how Millennials will vote in the coming decade. The average Democratic legislator may approach Millennial-centric issues with more sympathy than Republican lawmakers, but as a party, the Democrats are not quite the Millennial patron saints they fancy themselves to be. More than a handful of Democratic Representatives and Senators have consistently voted against tighter emissions regulations and fracking restrictions, both of which would ultimately serve to protect the environment.[4] The party has been late to the game in recognizing the severity of the student loan bubble—it took Hillary Clinton until August of 2016 to publicly offer ideas that might save indebted students from a trip to the bankruptcy court further down the road.[5] (And these ideas did little to address the rising cost of

---

[4] Democrats like Joe Manchin, who reside in states that rely upon coal-fired power plants, often find themselves in the bind of paying lip service to environmental advocates while downplaying local anxieties about energy reform killing jobs. But this will do little to elicit sympathy from Millennials worried about rising oceans and years-long heat waves.

[5] Clinton's "New College Compact" would allow students to attend an in-state public university without taking out loans. It's an important proposal, but it came too late to win the trust and fervor of a vast majority of Millennials.

education in America.) When President Obama tried to add a public option to the Affordable Care Act—a move that was widely supported by Obama's Millennial supporters—a coalition of Republican *and* Democratic lawmakers assembled to protect the health insurance sector, forcing Obama to abandon the public option.

What we know now, in the wake of Hillary Clinton's failed presidential campaign, is that driving mass Millennial turnout on Election Day is not as simple as offering fine-tuned talking points that merely acknowledge issues like climate change or campaign finance reform. Nor will it be as convenient as taking a middle-of-the-road approach to addressing these issues.

First and foremost, those who seek the average Millennial voter's trust must possess a record of serviceable action that consistently reflects their values—a certificate of "realness," if you will. Most Millennials are young enough to have only seen Washington DC at its most craven and dysfunctional. One of the more unique things that Bernie Sanders offered his Millennial-rich base was a political career characterized by bold positions on economic fairness, environmental preservation, and social justice. These were the same principal issues that Sanders campaigned on. They are, to this day, his brand. Is it realistic to hold *all* politicians to such a high standard, in appraising their authenticity? Maybe, maybe not, but either way, Sanders' ascension as a political superstar and the memory of his presence in the 2016 race appear to be changing the way that young people evaluate candidates and incumbent officials. Having been introduced to a politician who truly "walks the walk and "talks the talk," most Millennials will not be amenable to the likely establishment argument that the integrity of Bernie Sanders is a rare quality to expect from the average elected official—especially since the average American's desire for political integrity will likely grow under President Trump, who has already broken campaign promises such as providing affordable health coverage for all Americans, or strong-arming Mexico into paying for his proposed wall.

Once trust is established between Millennials and someone with the audacity to ask for their votes, the next step is to look forward and propose bigger, bolder, and more high-concept solutions to problems that have exacerbated the Millennial generation's collective frustrations. Anything less—especially coming from Baby Boomer or Generation X'er politicians—can offer the impression that the magnitude of concern felt by so many Millennial voters, with respect to any issue, is not shared their elected representatives. This fractured dynamic between the nervous, vulnerable voter and the out-of-touch political class is exactly what turned the 2016 U.S. election into a brawl between establishment politics, progressive populism, and the more nativist variety that Donald Trump leveraged to win the race. Nothing about Trump's platform was subtle or pragmatic, and I am not for a second suggesting that political parties should offer Millennials grandiose promises like suspending all fossil fuel production within one years, or converting America into a money-free society like the one Gene Roddenberry envisioned for *Star Trek*. But the key word in that last sentence is "envision." At a minimum, every generation needs something to dream of. If our political class offers Millennials insufficient hope that America might finally curb its carbon emissions or amplify the will of ordinary voters by placing limits on corporate campaign contributions, what reason do Millennials have to support either of the two "viable" political parties that control Washington DC?

What both major parties forget or fail to understand is that Millennials are young enough to have sharp memories. They may only be discovering their political power as a the largest living generation in America, but when it comes to the negotiations and deals that occur on Capitol Hill, Millennials are paying attention. (Most of them learned how to use Google before they were old enough to vote.) This could explain why in 2016, roughly one month from Election Day, more than 30% of Millennial voters surveyed declared that rather than vote for Hillary Clinton, who beat Millennial favorite Bernie Sanders for the Democratic nomination, they planned to support third party candidates—even if doing so would boost Donald Trump's odds of occupying the Oval Office. While the 2016 exit polls revealed that the third party crossover wasn't quite so high, the fact that so many Millennials were seriously tempted to leap into uncharted political waters prowled by the likes of Jill Stein and Gary Johnson should give heartburn to every Democratic and Republican party official.

What happens next depends on two things: President Trump's first year, and how the Democratic Party responds.

THE FUTURE

It is difficult to understate how much the Trump agenda resembles an act of generational warfare against Millennials. Between denying mankind's role in global warming, promoting bigotry and xenophobia with draconian immigration bills, giving states the green light to roll back laws that protect LGBTQ and reproductive rights, and cutting taxes for his oligarch buddies, Trump has displayed almost no interest in endearing himself to the majority of young voters. His allies—Jeff Sessions, Newt Gingrich, Rudy Giuliani, Sarah Palin, Ted Nugent—are refurbished products of from our cultural past. All are known for espousing viewpoints that clash sharply with those that inspired millions of Millennials to support Barack Obama's two presidential campaigns. Trump's unlikely presidency can sometimes appear to be the panicked scream of an older generation keenly aware of its mortality and impending expiration. If the adage that a dying mule kicks the hardest is applicable to this situation, then we can expect the Trump administration to aggressively pursue legislation that disempowers the young, whether it's new laws that will make it more cumbersome for young adults to vote, or social welfare reform that deprives Millennials and those to come from enjoying the benefits of Social Security or Medicare. These actions and the suffering they would cause could "activate" the Millennial generation in a manner that we haven't witnessed before.

Acts of Millennial-led resistance will likely occur at a party level and take root in small town America. Right now, no group is better positioned to benefit from a Millennial awakening than the Democrats. If the party is willing to rebuild itself by embracing grassroots fundraising methods, listening to younger leaders with fresh ideas, and offering all voters a more ambitious vision for the future—as Obama did on the campaign trail in 2008—Millennials could become the next Democratic firewall. It will be several years before most Millennials are eligible to run for Senate seats, but this hasn't stopped a handful of civically minded young adults from getting involved with their local government. Starting small has proved an effective electoral strategy for the growing number of Millennials that held some form of public office since the year 2015. Not just Mayor

Alex Morse of Holyoke, Massachusetts, but Ohio State Representative Emilia Sykes, who ran a campaign that spotlit debt and inequality, or Maine State Representative Ryan Fecteau, the youngest LGBTQ state representative in the nation. Towns and cities with large youth populations are the most likely proving grounds for Millennial-aged lawmakers, though I expect those in smaller locales will enjoy far greater success. Big cities tend to draw transient young professionals, and today's skyrocketing real estate prices in urban areas incentivize apartment hopping, often from one district to another. Small cities and towns are where most people go to settle down for at least a few years, if not forever. As Wesley, the former political organizer from Florida pointed out during our conversation, it's tough to engage in any local political scene when your mailing address is constantly changing. He would know, having moved annually for the past 15 years.

Now, what happens if the Democratic Party refuses to reinvent itself and instead doubles down on "safe" centrist policies and Super PAC-driven campaign funding? I predict that we'll witness a Millennial exodus from the party. (The Millennial exodus from the Republican Party has been ongoing for the past several years and will continue as long as Trump is in office.) Most of these young turks will likely re-register as Independents and throw in their lot with candidates that best embody the values shared by most Millennials. The parties that stand to benefit from this exodus, at this moment, are the Green Party and the Libertarian Party. But I wouldn't put it past Millennials to take a more entrepreneurial approach and form a new party that's better equipped to represent the Millennial generation's diversity of identity and experience. Robert Reich, the prominent UC Berkeley public policy professor and former Treasury Secretary, has suggested this idea in several of his viral Facebook posts. And the Icelandic comedian Jón Gnarr has provided a helpful playbook: in 2009, as a joke, he founded the "Best Party" amid nationwide political unrest and was subsequently elected Mayor of Reykjavik. If the exodus is massive enough, and Trump's presidency tempestuous enough, anything could happen.

Whatever comes to pass, wherever it is that Millennials, their offspring, and the next generations are going, the road that stretches beyond today will be long and treacherous. It would be dishonest and irresponsible of me to close this book by suggesting that everything will be alright—that Millennials will somehow find the right balance of pluck and luck to lead America into a more prosperous future. To make this happen, Millennials will have to fight for representation in a political class that has been unwilling to accommodate their interests and ideas. This will mean voting, in far greater numbers, and not just during the presidential elections. It will require hundreds, if not thousands of Millennials to consider themselves fit for public office and find the courage to ask their neighbors for their money and votes. (This will be especially taxing for Millennials who lack the cushion of an upper middle class community.) Above all, Millennials will have to decide for themselves if the American political system is something that can be salvaged, or whether people would be better off moving to Mars when Elon Musk's SpaceX begins offering starter homes to the first wave of colonists.

Speaking as a Millennial with six years worth of experience complaining about the way things are in America and imagining how they should be—usually out loud—I find it difficult to imagine a more horrendous fate than living in an intergalactic terrarium with neighbors who don't believe in the efficacy of voting or government by the people. What would we do when technical problems with the oxygenation system arose? Who would determine our course of action when our Year One food supply ran short before August? Even in the absence of a catastrophe, how do we channel our daily vexations into something more constructive than calling each other names and hitting each other with rocks?

It's time to answer that last question. Right here.

Right now.

BIBLIOGRAPHY

Allen, Jonathan & Parnes, Amy. *Shattered: Inside Hillary Clinton's Doomed Campaign.* New York: Crown Publishing Group, 2017.

Ballhaus, Rebecca & Zitner, Aaron. "Millennials Have Cooled on Hillary Clinton, Forcing a Campaign Reset." *Wall Street Journal.* September 16, 2016.

Borchers, Callum. "We need more questions like this one from Jake Tapper to Debbie Wasserman Schultz." *Washington Post.* February 12, 2016.

Cushing, Ellen. "The Bacon-Wrapped Economy." *East Bay Express.* March 20, 2013.

Foreman, Christopher H. "The Clash of Purposes: Environmental Justice and Risk Assessment." *Brookings.* March 20, 1998.

Gaudiano, Nicole. "Bernie Sanders defied expectations with long-shot presidential campaign." *USA Today.* July 11, 2016.

Glum, Julia. "Election Results 2014: At 21.3 Percent, Millennial Turnout About The Same As In Previous Midterms." *International Business Times.* November 5, 2014.

Gnarr, Jón. *Gnarr! How I Became the Mayor of a Large City in Iceland and Changed the World.* New York: Melville House, 2014.

Hais, Michael & Winograd, Morley. "President Obama, the

millennial whisperer." *Los Angeles Times.* January 16, 2017.

Howe, Neil & Strauss, William. *Millennials Rising: The Next Great Generation.* New York: Vintage Books, 2000.

Klein, Naomi. *This Changes Everything: Capitalism vs. The Climate.* New York: Simon & Schuster, 2015.

Kozlowska, Hanna. "Clint Eastwood gets Trump: 'When I grew up, those things weren't called racist.'" *Quartz.* August 16, 2016.

Lewin, Tamar. "Student-Loan Borrowers Average $26,500 in Debt." *New York Times.* October 18, 2012.

Malone, Scott. "Trump? Clinton? Many young Americans prefer giant meteor, poll finds." *Reuters.* October 18, 2016. McGreal, Chris. "Why Joe Lieberman is holding Barack Obama to ransom over healthcare." *The Guardian.* December 16, 2009.

Saegert, Rhiannon. "Natural gas well explodes in Denton." *North Texas Daily.* May 7, 2015.

Saulny, Susan. "After Recession, More Young Adults Are Living on Street." *New York Times.* December 18, 2012.

Seitz-Wald, Alex. "Clinton Adopts Key Piece of Sanders Student Debt Plan." *NBC News.* July 6, 2016.

Silva, Jennifer M. *Coming Up Short: Working-Class Adulthood in an Age of Uncertainty.* Oxford: Oxford University Press, 2015.

Stein, Jeff. "Study: Hillary Clinton's TV ads were almost entirely policy-free." *Vox.* March 8, 2017.

Taibbi, Matt. *Insane Clown President: Dispatches from the 2016 Circus.* New York: Spiegel & Grau, 2017.

ACKNOWLEDGEMENTS

There are not enough words of love and gratitude that can be offered to thank my parents, Brett Cook and Richard Howard, for their support throughout this project and long before it. Mom, Dad—knowing that you believed in my abilities as a storyteller as early as age five, when I took to drawing werewolf comics during recess, while the other kids played football, has been nothing short of integral to my development as a human being. I am absurdly fortunate to have the two of you in my life, and I love that we can talk about economic policy, Werner Herzog movies, and dick jokes over a singular meal or coffee.

Still, when tackling a project like this, there are some things that can only be discussed Millennial-to-Millennial, and my sister, Julia Howard, provided many valuable insights and ideas when I ran into walls during the production process. She also made that process more comfortable by taking me out for burgers and beers, putting me up during my travels, and at one point, letting me borrow her car so that I could travel deep into rural Oregon and interview a group of middle-aged forest dwellers. (That's for my next book.) I love you, Jules.

Getting older has made me appreciate what a privilege it is to come from a bug-nuts crazy family of creators and free thinkers with a mile-wide humanistic streak. Julie and Chris Cook, Margaret Howard, Hope Zanes, Jorden Cook, Jay Schadler, Silas Cook, Leslie Congleton, Trigger Cook, Mary Dilles, Esther Cook, Christine Eudoxie, Jane and Gary Robinson, Jenny and Al James, Ryland Cook, Aidan Pilgrim, Pearl Cook, Leslie and Jon Kremer, Kristen and Dave McDermott, Warren Zanes, Dan Zanes, Julie Zanes, Donald Saaf, Hank Nichols, and Nathan Nichols, I hope you know that our conversations and collective exploits have expanded my curiosity for all of the years that we've known each other.

Countless teachers, occupational and spiritual, have similarly nudged me towards a life of inquiry and creativity. The lion's share of credit goes to Drew Casper, John Waddell, Chris Freeman, Judy Hession, Cecilia Woloch, Tom Lester, Gerard Skinder, Mark Irwin, Lorin Maloney, Jon Wagner, Harold Apter, Vicki Forman, Chris Kurhajetz, Marguerite Maserian, Elvira Borsari, Jason Van Dinter, and finally, the inimitable Maura Albert.

Learning how to have a substantive conversation with anyone is something that must be learned. In this regard, I made my bones working in the Appalachian Mountain Club's high mountain huts as a cash-strapped college student. Mike Kautz, thank you for hiring me. Eric Pedersen, Jesse Billingham, and James Wrigley, thank you for letting me come back each subsequent summer. And of course, many thanks are due to my dear "croo" cohorts, George Heinrichs, Johannes Griesshammer, Iona Woolmington, Scott Berkley, Corlis Gross, Amy Aloe, Anne Weisheipl, Emma Leonard, Shelley Goulder, Courtney Wrigley, Sarah Brockett, Leah Hart, Uli Botzojorns, Mary Ann Weiss, Caroline Woolmington, Nate Brown, Betsy Cook, Cameron Berube, Thad Houston, Meredith Perkins, Beth Weick, Ari Ofsevit, Benny Taylor, Avery Anderson, Jamie Van Leuven, Nick Anderson, Ben Egan, and Grace Pezzella

Learning how to transform a substantive conversation into a story is also something that must be learned. My deepest thanks to Scott Kearnan, Jacqueline Houton, and Carly Carioli for giving me a first shot at turning that art form into a career. Additional thanks to Alex Tilsley, Asher Feldman, Eva Recinos, and Sean Fitz-Gerald for helping me realize that passion for storytelling as a student newspaper editor. I'll never forget ordering takeout dinner in a Roberto Benigni voice with the four of you there in the newsroom, listening and failing to suppress your laughter.

The idea that I could write a book that people might buy was not something that crossed my mind until 2011, when I met Martha Sullivan for a round of drinks on a cold winter's night in Boston. Martha, the whiskey was warming, but the conversation was life-changing.

That said, this book would never have happened if I didn't have the ability to support myself as a freelance writer, and the flexibility that comes with such a life. I will always be grateful to Mari Badger, Jay Heinrichs, Stefan Lanfer, JK Nickell, and Gina Nebesar for helping me take my editorial game to the next level, and beyond.

The production of *The Early Voters*, from a half-baked idea to a finished book, involved many kind, helpful individuals whom I'll list here.

First and foremost, my "on the road" crew. For all the meals, drinks, rides, laughs, and comfortable surfaces on which to sleep, thanks to Jack Meighan, John Facendola, Sam Oglesby, Kate Mitchell, Mary Weir, Zak Silverman, Brian Gillis, Amie Fleming, Ben Miller, Elizabeth Waste, Kelli Barr, Mickey Hartz, Shannon Wymer, Michele Miklos, Taichi Shinohara, Jon Branden, Alex MacPhail, Julie and Gregory Chun, Hillary Costa, Lincoln Fishman, Margaret Kizzler, Gina Shaw, Austin Kopack, Jen Krassler, Corey Costa, Veronica Morra, An Nguyen, Annabelle Hicks, Carol Fraser, Dorian Scheidt, Andy Parsons, Nick Chambers, Jon and Kem Sawyer, Jamie Barilone, Lincoln Benedict, Jess Marion, and Michael Larson.

Next, my post-production hosts. This book was written over the course of three years, in a rich variety of venues. Many of those writing venues were also home for short periods of time, and for that convenience and stability - a godsend when you're producing a book - I must thank Brian Fitzgerald, Stephanie Turnbull, Doug and Alice Fleer, Jonathan Meath, Doug and Alice Fleer, Shepley Metcalf, Reed Cochran, Clayton Spencer, and Jill Teitelman.

Editing takes more than one set of eyes, not to mention, honesty and imagination. I'm grateful for the assistance of Ronald Goldfarb, Sally Koslow, and Laura Caspian.

Self-publishing is a long and cumbersome journey, and my friend Sabrina Dax kindly helped me find a path through the editorial wilderness.

Finally, I will be eternally grateful for the company of every Millennial-aged adult who spoke with me for this book. To ask a stranger to lay bare intimate details of their lives puts both parties in a vulnerable position, but the interviewer shares only a small portion of that vulnerability. I applaud and thank all of my Millennial interview partners for their temerity, their generosity, and their eloquence. Talking with all of you about your lives was not only an honor and a joy—it was an effective form of therapy as I reconciled my own tribulations and anxieties as a Millennial.

RECOMMENDED READING

Few Millennial experts have monitored the growth of this generation more studiously than Neil Howe and William Strauss. Their book, *Millennials Rising: The Next Great Generation* is required reading for anyone that wants to learn more about who Millennials are. Whereas my book is the culmination of three years' worth of interviews, Howe and Strauss have been documenting the young adult experience for decades, and they haven't shown any sign of slowing down.

An insightful and criminally under-recognized book about the Millennial experience is Jennifer M. Silva's *Coming Up Short: Working-Class Adulthood in an Age of Uncertainty*. Most of the Millennial articles we see ("Top 15 Cities for Millennials" or "How Millennials Are Disrupting Burrito Bars") chronicle the experiences of a very specific subset of young adults—the upper-middle class. Silva digs deeper and humanizes Millennials who've *really* been left behind by the post-recession economy. Her book was a strong influence on *The Early Voters* and the manner in which I tracked down Millennial interview partners.

Lots of Millennials consume the majority of their media online, and I'm no exception. In a seemingly limitless sea of journalists and writers, an illustrious few have emerged as experts at covering the issues that lie at the heart of this book. Their writing is intelligent, illuminating, and passionate. For the curious and the civic-minded, I highly recommend tracking down the published works of Michelle Alexander, Ari Berman, Charles Bethea, Sam Biddle, Paul Blest, Clio Chang, Ta-Nehisi Coates, Ellen Cushing, Chris Faraone, Crystal Marie Fleming, Conor Friedersdorf, Thomas Frank, Sarah Jones, Shaun King, Naomi Klein, Drew Magary, Sean McElwee, Hamilton Nolan, George Packer, Alex Pareene, Eve Peyser, Jason Pramas, Symone Sanders, Jon Schwarz, Jia Tolentino, and especially Adam Weinstein.

Finally, I owe a serious debt to the late Studs Terkel and his landmark book, *Working: People Talk About What They Do All Day and How They Feel About What They Do*. No literary work influenced my book more profoundly than Terkel's. I implore you to experience his masterpiece.

MILES HOWARD is an author, editor, and political researcher whose work has been featured in the Boston Phoenix, Southwest: The Magazine, The Hill, and the Los Angeles Times. He is a regular contributor to NPR's WBUR Boston and a graduate of the University of Southern California. His next book, *Red Sky at Night*, will arrive in early 2018.